The Flavors of Iraq

Impressions of My Vanished Homeland

Feurat Alani

Illustrated by Léonard Cohen

Translated by Kendra Boileau

Foreword by Ross Caputi

Graphic Mundi

Library of Congress Cataloging-in-Publication Data

Names: Alani, Feurat, 1980– author. | Cohen, Léonard, 1982– illustrator. |
Boileau, Kendra, translator.
Title: The flavors of Iraq : impressions of my vanished homeland / Feurat Alani ;
illustrated by Léonard Cohen ; translated by Kendra Boileau.
Other titles: Parfum d'Irak. English
Description: University Park, Pennsylvania : Graphic Mundi, [2024] | Translation
of Le parfum d'Irak.
Summary: "A graphic memoir recounting the author's childhood in Iraq and
his experiences during the Iraq War and its aftermath from 1989 to 2011"—
Provided by publisher.
Identifiers: LCCN 2023052061 | ISBN 9781637790670 (paperback)
Subjects: LCSH: Alani, Feurat, 1980-—Comic books, strips, etc. | Iraq War,
2003–2011—Personal narratives—Comic books, strips, etc. | Iraq War, 2003–
2011—Journalists—Biography—Comic books, strips, etc. | Journalists—
France—Biography—Comic books, strips, etc. | Iraq—History—Comic books,
strips, etc. | Iraq—Social life and customs—Comic books, strips, etc. | LCGFT:
Autobiographical comics. | Graphic novels. | Nonfiction comics. | War comics.
Classification: LCC DS79.766.A53 A3 2024 | DDC 956.7044/3092 [B]—dc23/
eng/20231208
LC record available at https://lccn.loc.gov/2023052061

Printed in Türkiye
Published by The Pennsylvania State University Press,
University Park, PA 16802–1003

Originally published as *Le Parfum d'Irak*, copyright © 2018 Éditions Nova,
© Arte Éditions.
This edition published by arrangement with Marotte et Compagnie Agence
Littéraire in conjunction with their duly appointed co-agent Agence Deborah
Druba, Paris, France. All rights reserved.

Graphic Design by Yoann De Roeck.

10 9 8 7 6 5 4 3 2 1

graphic mundi
drawing our worlds together

Graphic Mundi is an imprint of The Pennsylvania State University Press.

The Pennsylvania State University Press is a member of the Association of
University Presses.

It is the policy of The Pennsylvania State University Press to use acid-free paper.
Publications on uncoated stock satisfy the minimum requirements of American
National Standard for Information Sciences—Permanence of Paper for Printed
Library Material, ANSI Z39.48-1992.

Foreword

I first met Feurat Alani in the spring of 2011. I was living in Boston, working through the final semester of my undergraduate studies. But rather than cramming for exams, I was mostly busy protesting and speaking out against the occupation of Iraq.

Since I got out of the Marine Corps in 2006, I felt I owed a moral debt to Iraqis, and to the city of Fallujah in particular. Though it still stings to admit it, I was part of the assault force that laid siege to Fallujah in late 2004. Over the course of a month, we turned the entire city to rubble and left an estimated 4,000–6,000 civilians dead in our wake. I know the damage can't be undone, nor the debt repaid. But as an acknowledgment of wrongdoing and a gesture of remorse, I committed myself to campaigning for withdrawal and reparations.

It was no easy thing knowing just how wrong what we did was and struggling so much to convince the American public of it. I tried everything within my means: attending marches and protests, organizing speaking events and teach-ins, and telling my story about how I, a former marine, came to oppose the war to anyone who would listen. The problem was that the only people who wanted to listen were those who already agreed with me. Such is the case with activism sometimes. Those who need to know don't care, and those who care already know.

So, when I received an email from Feurat Alani requesting an interview and explaining that he had a contract with a major French television network to make a documentary film about Fallujah, I saw it as a rare opportunity to speak to a mainstream audience. I accepted immediately.

I knew nothing about Feurat at the time except that he had an Iraqi name. Assuming that he had lived, or might still be living, in Iraq, I prepared myself to face the scorn and contempt that I expected him to feel toward his former occupier. If it helped raise awareness, I was willing to be grilled in front of the camera. Only Feurat never grilled me. There was not a bit of condemnation in his attitude toward me. In fact, he didn't limit himself to recording my testimony but presented me in his film as someone committed to the truth.

That was my first impression of Feurat. The grace with which he treated me spoke not only to his kindness but to the depth of his understanding of the global forces—political, economic, and cultural—that brought a kid from middle-of-nowhere Massachusetts to his parents' hometown in Iraq.

Thus began a long friendship and collaboration. And not only on issues regarding Iraq. It turns out we had a lot in common. We were both old-school, observant of the traditions of our respective backgrounds—me Italian and him Iraqi. We shared an appreciation for '90s-era rap and a commitment to fitness and martial arts that bordered on obsession. I joked with him about my white trash roots, and he joked about his ghetto youth on the outskirts of Paris. When he came to the US years later, he stayed at my house. And when I visited Paris, I stayed at his. He even introduced me to his father.

It has been a bromance for the ages. Though his boxing skills may be inferior to mine, and I am clearly the better looking of the two, Feurat has otherwise become like a big brother to me. I regard him as senior in all things, but especially writing. I've learned so much from him about storytelling and digital media. But if I could boil his insights down to a single maxim, it's this: Tell the human story.

It's no accident that this is exactly what's been missing from our popular understanding of Iraq. Over the last twenty years, the story of the invasion and occupation has been told almost exclusively from an American perspective that is so full of myth and omission that the entire collection of novels, films, memoirs, and journalistic accounts belongs in the fantasy genre. Not only are they historically inaccurate across the board, but they also share a common narrative form. American soldiers are the protagonists of these stories. To the extent that Iraqis are included at all, it is either as victims or villains; and, in either case, the need for Americans to save the day is implicit. According to this narrative, the invasion is not an act of aggression but an attempted liberation gone wrong. Consequently, the conflict is driven by anti-American insurgents and religious extremists who seek to undermine our well-intended nation-building project, not by the actions of a foreign invader attempting to impose a very limited form of democracy, ironically, without popular consent or participation.

If Iraq through American eyes seems more the product of wishful thinking than reality, it's because the framing, omissions, and narrative tropes that have characterized much of the fiction and nonfiction on Iraq have flowed downstream from US military propaganda. One of the lesser-known aspects of Operation Iraqi Freedom is that the way the story was told—the controlled perspective, the characterization of the actors involved, the focus on strategic themes, the tactical use of language—was as much a part of the battle plan as was the use of bombs and infantry. New trends in strategic thinking at the turn of the millennium gave propaganda a more prominent role in American military operations during the global war on terror. Soft power, it was believed, would allow the military to win the hearts and minds of Iraqis, reducing the need for deadly force. It didn't actually work out that way. But the fact that our propaganda operations remain a lesser-known aspect of the war speaks to their success in constructing a popular (mis)understanding of the conflict that has been reproduced again and again in American pop culture.

This has been possible at least in part because propaganda has grown increasingly inconspicuous over the years. No longer the opaque Uncle Sam posters of WWI, propaganda today, to the untrained eye, would be nearly indistinguishable from news. Of course, no one calls it propaganda anymore. The US military coordinates a set of activities (that can only be described as propaganda) under the rubric of *information operations*. In Iraq this involved sponsoring US-friendly, Arabic-language news media companies and creating press information centers where American military spokespersons could offer choreographed accounts of our actions directly to the media. Perhaps their most cunning and discrete method of propaganda was the use of embedded journalists. The US military offered journalists access to the battlefield, if they allowed themselves to be chaperoned by a platoon. However, this clever tactic afforded the US military greater control over the perspective from which Americans would learn about the occupation by foregrounding the experiences of American soldiers and relegating the experiences of Iraqis to the background.

From *The Hurt Locker* (2008) to *American Sniper* (2014) and *The Yellow Birds* (2012), American pop culture has followed the model set by US information operations, pumping out story after story told through the familiar gaze of the American soldier. No matter that the invasion was a war crime. No matter that over a million Iraqis died in the course of the occupation. All ethical questions about the mission are, at most, a secondary plotline. And Iraq and Iraqis are just a setting in these stories about American soldiers and their struggles to heal the wounds of war.

The Flavors of Iraq is a refreshing break from this model. But its virtue is more than just a shift in perspective. *Flavors* offers an embodied narrative, rich in sensory experience. Feurat invites us to follow him through his childhood trips to visit family while Iraq was under sanctions and also through his later work as a journalist during the occupation with all the smells, tastes, and emotions of daily life. It's a story grounded in the intimacy of the human experience. It's rich in details that no outsider could ever know, like the taste of apricot ice cream in Baghdad or the danger of wearing a pair of Reebok Pumps in a country cut off from the rest of the world. It shows the full spectrum of the Iraqi experience over the last thirty years of conflict: death, destruction, disorder, and at the same time the warmth of family, the resilience of faith, and the comfort of good food.

And, while it is so much, it is also very little. *Flavors* is an exercise in minimalism. What began as a series of 1,000 tweets grew from its virality into an animated film with the brilliant illustrations of Léonard Cohen and, now, an international graphic novel. And perhaps its minimalist form is the point. How else could so little achieve so much if not for the simple power of empathy? There is something uniquely powerful about seeing through another's eyes and knowing what they felt down to the smells and sounds. There has to be something built into us, like a switch that once activated will suppress all tribalist impulses and allow you to just feel on a purely human level. Stories that pull us into the skin of others also pull us out of the abstractness of our ideological commitments and political affiliations and ground us in something more real.

After all, that's how I began to change. It wasn't from some activist pamphlet, but from the kindness and hospitality of the Iraqi people, even in the face of military aggression. It was the little details, the feel of Iraq. The brightness of the desert stars, unfaded by ambient light. The smell and taste of fresh bread baked in a rustic village kiln. The sun glistening off the Euphrates and the charm of the historic villages that checker its banks. It was the smells and tastes and impressions of a society that had hardship and tragedy heaped upon it from outside. It started there, with an appreciation for the beauty around me. Then curiosity grew. I wanted to see Iraq through Iraqi eyes, and that also meant looking at myself and my country through Iraqi eyes.

The Flavors of Iraq offers us just that—an opportunity to see Iraq through Iraqi eyes. And a rare opportunity it is. For the gulf between the American perception of our war and the Iraqi experience of it is as wide as the Anbar desert. And for too long, American cultural products on the war have offered us a mirror, rather than a bridge, reflecting our own self-image back to us. But now we have a bridge. It's there, if you care to look. On the other side awaits something new, a way of seeing and thinking that might be unfamiliar and challenging. But it's real. If you care to look, *The Flavors of Iraq* is the human story that we were never meant to see.

—Ross Caputi,
author of *The Sacking of Fallujah: A People's History*

Translator's Note

A graphic novel that juxtaposes illustrations with *tweets*? Critics don't always agree on what makes a graphic novel a graphic novel, and this book will most likely confirm that. When I read the French edition of *The Flavors of Iraq* (*Le parfum d'Irak*), I was hooked by Feurat Alani's narrative approach that threaded together one thousand tweets to tell his story. The original series of French tweets was pushed out into the Francophone Twittersphere from June to August 2016 and was subsequently edited for publication as a French graphic novel in 2018, shifting the significance of its tweet format from a practical means of communication to more of a narrative conceit.

When you think about it, this conceit works beautifully for this graphic novel. Not unlike the "gutters" in more conventional graphic novels (the blank space between illustrations that are often enclosed in "panels"), the narrative space between Alani's tweets is full of tension, of implied action or reflection. This transition space invites the reader to use their imagination to fill in the gaps in the narrative the way they would between the panels of a comic. These can be gaps in time—What has happened in the intervening days, months, or years between this tweet and the preceding one that the narrator hasn't described?—or even gaps in the author's memory, since the events at the time of narration happened a number of years ago.

The interspersed art by Léonard Cohen also affords space for the reader to wonder about what *hasn't* been depicted or said: a page here and there with three stacked art panels offers a nonverbal account of certain moments in the story, as do his dramatic two-page spreads and his evocative single splash pages. The juxtaposition of these different narrative elements, as well as the author's use of the historical present throughout, coalesce into a form that compels the reader to feel as if they're right there with the author *in real time*, engaged and invested in what the author terms a "counternarrative" to the "cold and analytic" mediated accounts of the geopolitical turmoil that befell Iraq from 1989 to 2011.

The lack of a broader context surrounding some of these tweets (the gaps I referred to above) made translating them a challenge at times. Here and there I have altered the text slightly to offer a small bit of context or clarity regarding the events in this story. I have tried to convey a distinctive authorial voice by focusing on rhythm and cadence in addition to word choice. And because language undergoes something called expansion and contraction over the course of translation, I have had to make very minor adjustments to the length of some of the tweets to accommodate the superb layout of this book by French graphic designer Yoann De Roeck. As you'll see, the text on facing pages aligns both at the top and the bottom.

Finally, a note on the translation of the title, *Le parfum d'Irak*. "Parfum" has a multivalence that "perfume" lacks in modern usage. Obviously, it signifies olfactory phenomena, and we know that smells made such an enormous impression on the author during his visits to his homeland (see tweet 730). But "parfum," too, can refer to flavors or tastes, such as the ice cream invoked early in the book having *le parfum d'abricot*, the taste of apricot. In needing to choose a term that related either to smell or to taste, I decided to go with the latter, hence, *Flavors of Iraq*, which to my mind metaphorically signifies a potential for the discovery of a multitude of distinctive features, traits, qualities, and characteristics that once defined Iraq. While this English translation is yet another step removed from the version of the text that appeared online quite a few years ago, my hope is that it will speak to readers with the same sense of immediacy that the French edition does, and that it will break down the barriers of culture, time, and space for an Anglophone audience that has largely been insulated from the details of this history.

—Kendra Boileau,
Publisher, Graphic Mundi

For Yasser

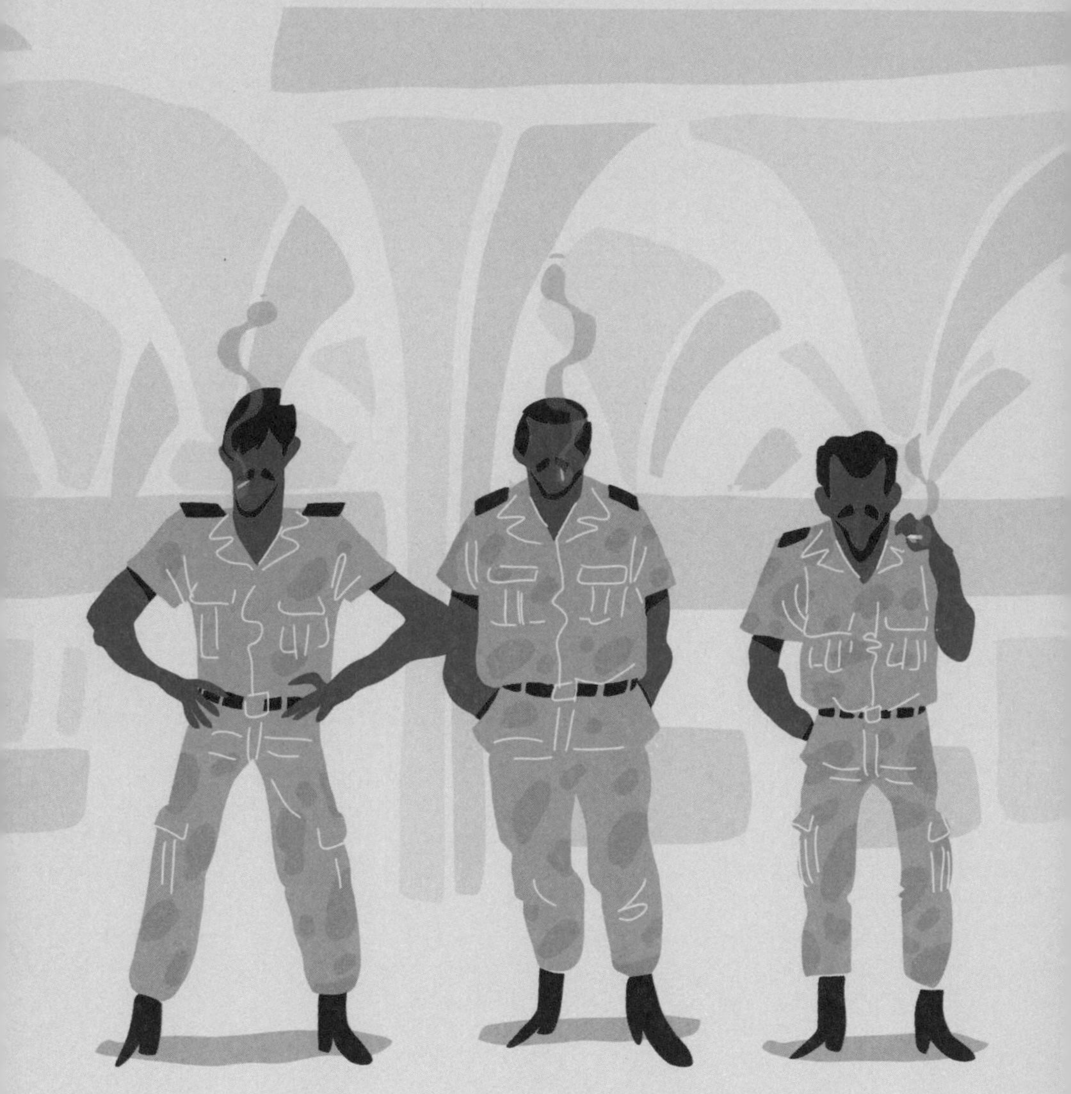

1989 My first trip to Iraq. The taste of apricot. "Never say Saddam's name."

Iran–Iraq War
In September 1980, Iraq invades Iran. The objectives are several. Iraq wants to "regain" the Khuzestan province of Iran, as well as the Shatt al-Arab River, which starts at the confluence of the Tigris and the Euphrates and runs for 200 kilometers before emptying into the Persian Gulf. It also wants to deal a fatal blow to the Islamic Revolution, which it believes is about to fall.

01 October 1989: The #IranIraqWar has ended. An Iraqi expat in France, my father decides to send us home for two months. I'm nine years old, and I'm finally going to see Iraq.

02 My father still can't go home. When he was younger, he was a political dissident. He's not sure if he can return home safely.

03 An Arab welcome at the Baghdad airport, where about 100 family members are waiting for us. I'm wearing a blue tie. I go from hug to hug.

04 My mother's side of the family lives in Baghdad in the districts of Mansour, Amiriya, Adhamiya, and Yarmouk. On my father's side, it's Fallujah, an "ordinary" city.

05 I notice three men who are mustached, stoic, and a little off to the side. They're wearing military uniforms. These are my three uncles from Fallujah.

06 In Baghdad I'm immediately struck by how modern the country is—the airport, Iraqi Airways, the highways, the streetlights, American cars.

07 The custom here is to visit the eldest relative first and move down to the youngest. So, Yarmouk first, then Mansour, then Amiriya. The houses are huge. Baghdad is magnificent.

Saddam Hussein
Iraqi statesman, born on April 28, 1937, in al-Awja, near Tikrit, and executed by hanging on December 30, 2006, in Baghdad. He was the president of the Republic of Iraq from 1978 to 2003.

08 My cousin whispers in my ear to never say the name of #SaddamHussein in the street. My six-year-old sister thought it was a game. She yells out his name.

09 My cousin jumps on us and shoves us into her car. On the way home, she's screaming at us. She's furious. This was a real eye-opener.

10 One week after our arrival in Baghdad, it's time to visit my uncles in Fallujah. They're expecting us. So, we head west!

11 On the road to Fallujah, I'm with three of my uncles, Imad, Ayad, and Riyad. All military. They spent eight years at war with Iran.

12 When we get to town, I notice the differences in infrastructure between Baghdad and Fallujah. I feel like I'm in the countryside.

13 We head for the blue-collar district of Jolan, which will become famous in 2004. . . . The house is simple and spacious with a chicken coop inside.

14 Uncle Riyad offers to take me for a drive along the Euphrates. The river is turquoise-blue. There's a green bridge constructed by the Brits.

Blackwater Private American military company founded by Erik Prince, which deployed soldiers in Iraq and Afghanistan. Earlier it was called "Blackwater Worldwide," and when it was founded it was known as "Blackwater USA." On February 12, 2009, the company was named "Xe," and then "ACADEMI," in December 2011.

15 This green bridge will also become famous in 2004. Four "lost" #Blackwater contractors will be killed and strung up at the entrance to the bridge.

16 We cross this bridge driving a *Barasili*. All officers in Fallujah have a Volkswagen Brasilia, a car for the masses.

17 We stop the car on the right bank. I'm bored. My uncle hands me his pistol. A real one. I stick it in my belt. Sometimes I wave it around . . .

18 Back in Jolan, I'm still bored. There are no toys. My uncle wiggles open the bullets from his revolver and spreads the black powder on the ground.

19 He flicks his lighter near the black powder. Sparks light up the kitchen. I think about my sister, who is probably eating ice cream in Baghdad.

20 My first visit to Fallujah gives me a new perspective on things. I realize how humbly my uncles live. And that there's some resentment toward Baghdad.

21 At night we sleep on the patio. The sky in Fallujah is clear. Donkeys bray, dogs bark, but I don't see the proverbial caravan.

22 The next morning, my uncle Riyad takes me to see a soccer game in a dirt stadium. Then we play pool in a game room for men only.

23 I meet my cousins. There's Ahmed, who looks like Mike Tyson. And there's Lubna, with dark hair and blue eyes. She's the daughter of my uncle Saad.

24 Uncle Saad walks with a limp. He lost half of his foot during the war with Iran. He receives state aid. Sitting next to him, my uncle Jamal laughs.

25 Uncle Jamal shot down an Iranian plane during the war. He even got a medal for it. I notice that my uncles all have gap teeth.

26 We go out to eat at the best restaurant in Fallujah: Haji Hussein, famous for its kebabs. All the truck drivers stop there.

27 Next we go to the *souk* downtown, near 40th Street. I discover the Arab market, dusty and noisy but entertaining.

28 A late lunch at the home of my father's mother-in-law, Samia. We sit on the ground to eat. She's the boss. The guys listen to her with devotion.

29 She pinches my cheeks, asks questions about my father, asks Uncle Jamal if she can have a look at the "list."

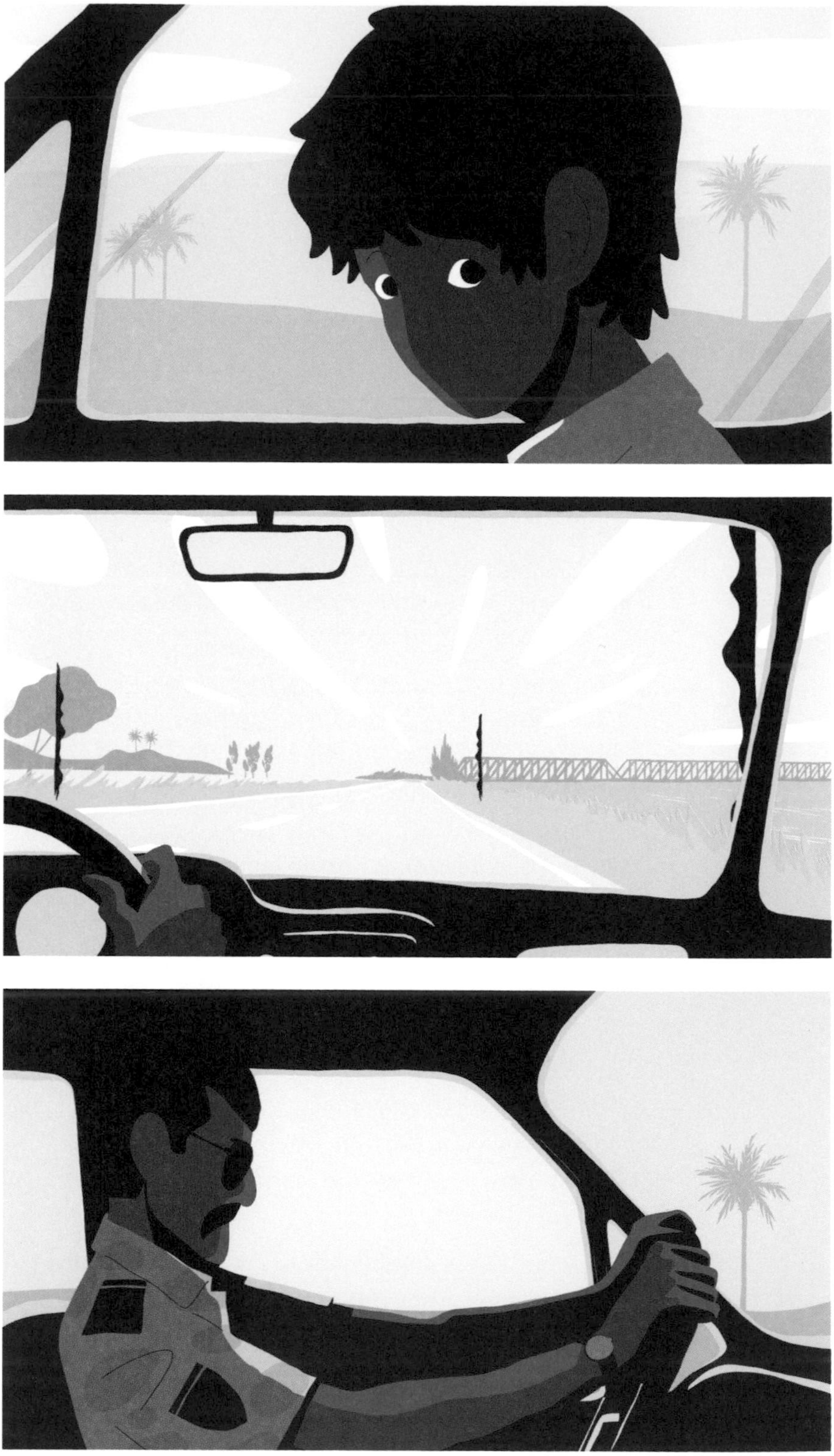

30 The list holds the names of Iraqi dissidents who fled the country. My father's name is on it. Maybe one day his name will be removed.

31 Some children in the Jolan district are curious and come to see me. They know I'm from abroad. They ask me questions about France.

Martyrs' Cemetery Once a soccer field for the Fallujah Sports Club, the area became an improvised burial ground after the First Battle of Fallujah in April 2004. Both soldiers and civilians are buried there. The cemetery holds about 3,000 graves.

32 We play soccer in a field near a mosque. No one could know that fifteen years later this playing field would become the #MartyrsCemetery.

33 I see Cousin Ahmed again. Because his father died, he can't go to school. He must work to support the family.

34 He works at the market, carrying boxes of vegetables all day long. In 2004, he'll carry boxes of weapons. It's his fate.

35 Poetry is the second national sport, after soccer. My uncle Imad is a poet and a writer. He drafts administrative documents for people who don't write.

Badr Shakir al-Sayyab بدر شاكر السياب (December 24, 1926–December 24, 1964) The indisputable standard for modern Arabic poetry and one of the founders of free verse in Arabic literature.

36 In the evenings, he likes to read his poems and those of #alSayyab. He also likes to issue the call to prayer. Out of the corner of his eye, he makes sure I'm watching. And listening.

37 Fallujah felt to me like a hard, traditional, and ordinary town. I was starting to get my bearings.

38 At nightfall, I felt the anxiety of a child who was used to city life. I liked the silence of the nighttime. The boredom, not so much.

39 After a week with my paternal uncles, returning to Baghdad was such a relief. It was shameful to feel this way when you saw their sad faces.

40 We say goodbye at the highway exit for Abu Ghraib. My cousin Ziad from the Mansour district is there. My uncles each raise a hand. "Fimallah," as they say here.

41 In Mansour, we stop to get ice cream. I taste one of the best ice creams of my entire life. Apricot flavor. The flavor of Baghdad.

42 The next day, we visit my maternal uncle Aziz on his farm. It's his vacation place. They're making *masgouf*, a regional carp dish.

43 Uncle Aziz is passionate about horses. He has a stable of Arabian purebloods. The people who take care of them are from Sudan and Egypt.

44 My Baghdadi cousins live better here than those in Fallujah. Sometimes I hear a tinge of irreverence in their comments. The city versus the countryside.

45 You see this kind of disdain even within Baghdad. The rich district of Mansour versus Amiriya, for example. A lot of people from Fallujah live in Amiriya, incidentally.

46 We come back from the farm. My father calls and reminds my sister and me about our schoolwork. It's the middle of the school year.

47 Cousin Selma lives in Baghdad but spent a couple years in Poitiers, France, earlier. She speaks French and teaches us one of our lessons. The one study day of our entire vacation.

48 We head to Mosul for the weekend, a favorite destination for Baghdadis at the time. The weather is cooler there. The local specialty: *mann al-sama.*

49 "Mann al-sama" means "manna from heaven." It's a kind of nougat with cardamom. I'll never forget how it tasted. I'll never forget Mosul.

50 We spend the rest of the summer between Baghdad and Fallujah. A summer I will never forget. The first encounter with my "roots," Iraq.

51 Back home in Paris, I rejoin my fourth-grade class. They call me "the ghost" because I disappeared for two months, with the principal's permission, of course.

52 My friends ask questions about Iraq. I tell them about Baghdad and Fallujah. Mme. Girard asks me to do a class presentation about it.

53 I talk mostly about Baghdad. They are surprised by my description of Iraq. Modern, and nothing like the clichés that even I had in mind.

54 The year ends pretty well for me. For my sister, it's more complicated. She's in first grade and is trying to get caught up in math.

55 August 1990. One of my aunts and some cousins from Baghdad come to visit us in France. Summer was just beginning. The nightmare, too.

56 On August 2, Saddam Hussein invades Kuwait. One cousin whoops with joy. Another one bursts into tears and says, prophetically: "This is the end of Iraq."

57 There's commotion at home. What will the response from the international community be like? My father foresees a fierce war and chaos unleashed.

58 The response is in fact one of unprecedented violence. Baghdad is bombarded. We sit watching the evening news on TV. Antiaircraft artillery rips through the sky.

59 My father's been drinking. He stands in front of the TV and yells "Be strong, my brothers!" I think about my uncles who have to fight now.

60 The first images appear of Iraqi soldiers taken as prisoners of war. I can't find the words to describe what I felt that day.

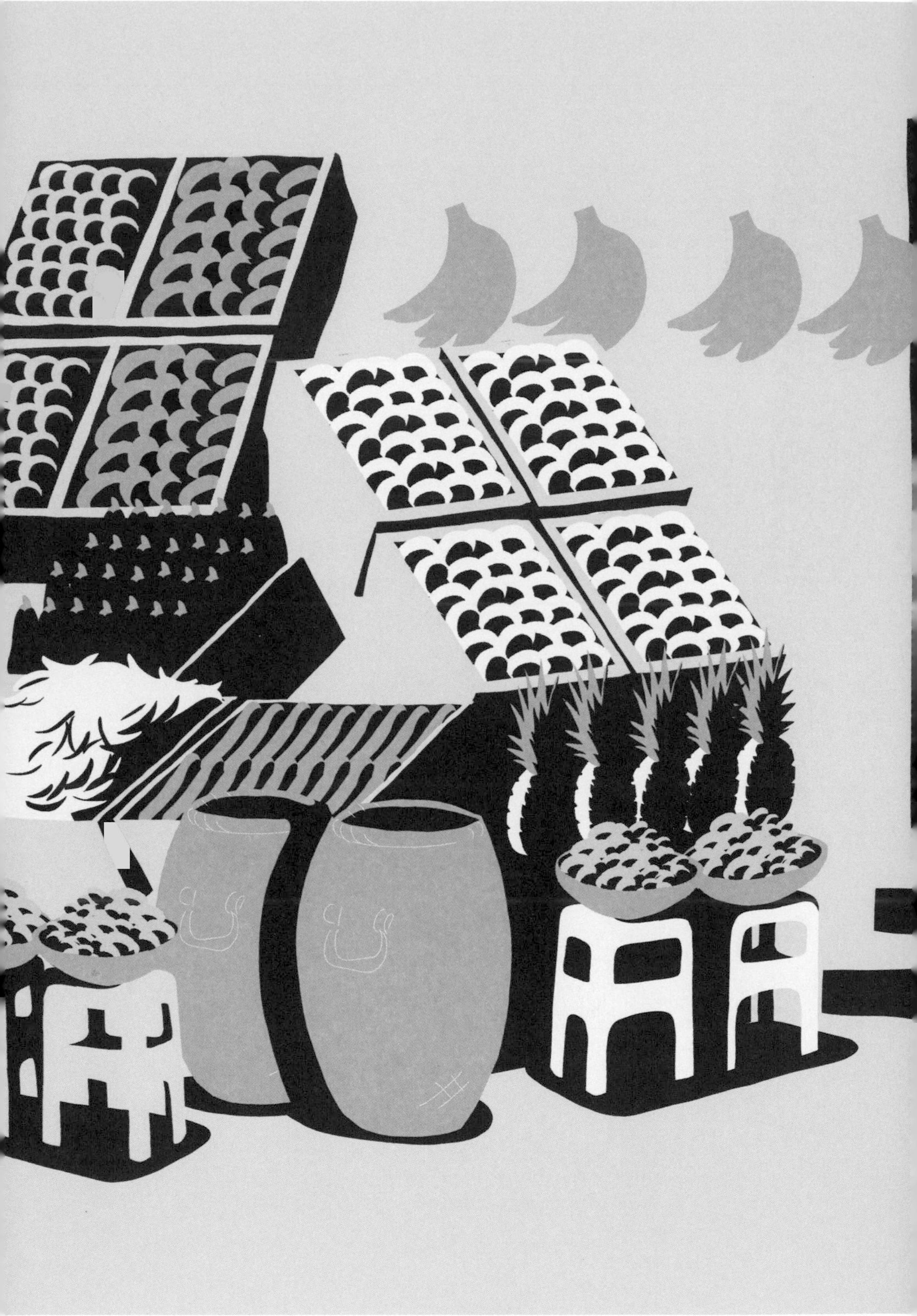

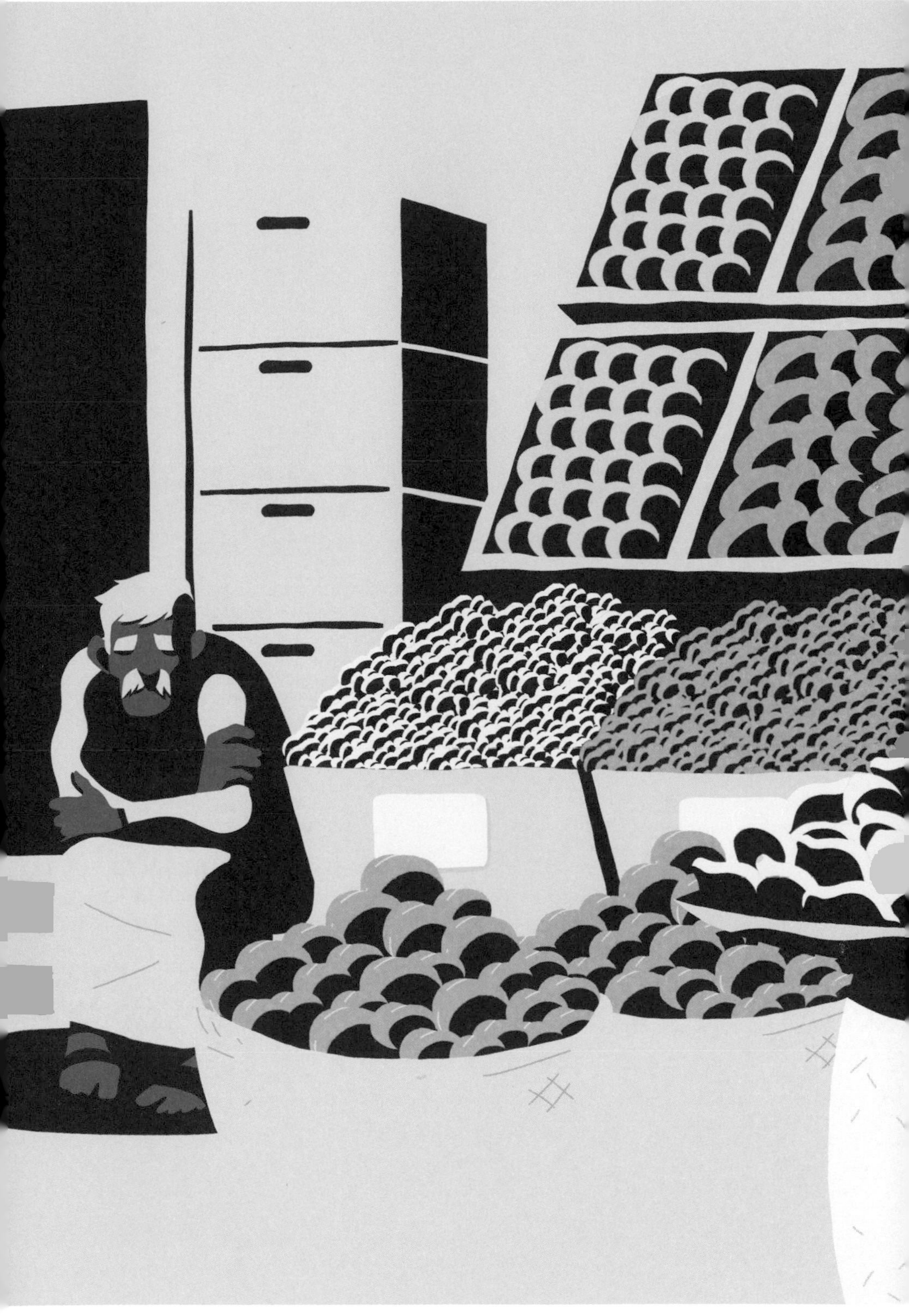

61 On the school playground the next day, everyone talks about the "fireworks" in the skies over Iraq. My classmates stare at me.

62 I'm the only Iraqi student there, obviously. I don't know how to deal with this. My friends are from North Africa and France. A conversation begins.

63 I discover how carelessly children choose their words. I'm afraid of their violence. Kader, who is from Morocco, will be the first to disappoint me.

64 Naively, I look for moral support from my Arab "brothers." But Kader gets off to a bad start. "Did you see the war on TV? It was like a movie. . . ."

65 He continues, "The Americans really screwed you over! It's the most powerful army in the world!" He laughs. Offended, I clench my fists.

66 I'm ten years old. It's the first time I fight over politics. The principal calls me to her office. I explain what happened.

67 She listens to me and then says she thinks a lot about Iraq. That she empathizes. Here is support I didn't dare hope for. Mme. Crespi smiles at me.

68 She'll come to my house on several occasions to hear how our family in Iraq is doing. She'll cry alongside my mother and my father.

69 One evening, my mother thinks she sees my cousin Mahmud among some Iraqi prisoners. The resemblance is remarkable. But fortunately, it's not him.

70 We move away and lose track of Mme. Crespi, the principal. Operation #DesertStorm is over. Thirty-six countries have destroyed mine.

Operation "Desert Storm" Military operation led by the United States as part of an international coalition commissioned by the United Nations against Iraq, from January 17 to February 28, 1991. The campaign put an end to Iraq's occupation of Kuwait. It was the most violent phase of the Gulf War.

71 I hear that the embargo imposed on Iraq is the harshest one ever. Three years have passed since my first trip there. In 1992, we go back. Again, without my father.

72 There's no longer a direct flight to Baghdad. We have to stop in Jordan and drive from there. We drive for twelve hours. I can feel Iraq getting closer.

73 In Trebil, at the Iraqi border, our 4×4 is thoroughly searched. We wait five hours before we get the green light from the #*Mukhabarat*.

Mukhabarat
جهاز المخابرات العامة العراقية
The Iraqi Intelligence Service (IIS) under Saddam Hussein, tasked with the collection and analysis of international intelligence, as well as secret police activities for the regime. It was dissolved by Paul Bremer in 2003.

74 Later, on the deserted road, we pass by Rutba, Ramadi, and Fallujah before we reach Baghdad at dawn. We park at my aunt's place in Mansour.

75 Not as many people greet us. The Mansour district is as beautiful as always, but the signs of war are there. I see a demolished bridge.

76 The embargo has done damage. The Iraqi dinar has plummeted. Medications are increasingly hard to find. But the Iraqis are rebuilding the city.

77 I reconnect with my cousins. It occurs to me that, while they have grown up in war and fear, I've been safe in Paris. It's a dose of reality.

78 We head out into the streets of Mansour, my sister, Hasna, Mazen, and I, to go buy candy. We enter a small shop.

79 Much to our consternation, there are no chocolates, none of the wonderful candies we found in 1989. No Bounty, no Mars, no KitKat bars.

80 Iraq can no longer import sugar. The candies we found were dates wrapped in paper. My sister bursts into tears.

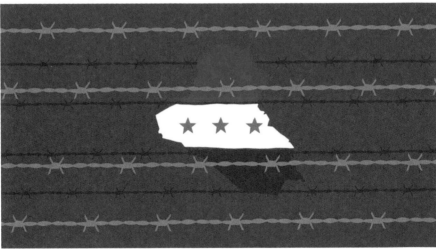

81 The treats that seemed boring to us in 1989 were gone. No more chocolate, no more ice cream. There are power outages. It's hot. The whole thing is a shock.

Amiriya Shelter
ملجأ العامرية
Shelter destroyed by the American Air Force during the Gulf War.

82 We are at my aunt's house in Khamael in the Amiriya district in western Baghdad. I spot the children I met here in 1989.

83 At dusk, we're playing soccer in the street. Everyone is barefoot except me. I kick the ball clumsily, and it hits a cyclist. He falls off his bike.

84 When I go to apologize, I recognize his face. It's the gentleman who worked at the Fallujah market in 1989. Since then, a lot of people have settled here.

85 After soccer, the children tell me about the sirens. The bombings. The escape to small towns. And the shelter that was bombed in this district.

86 On February 13, 1991, 408 women and children sheltering in the #AmiriyaShelter were incinerated by two Tomahawk missiles.

87 Among the victims were my great aunt and her granddaughter. The shelter has since become a memorial to those who died there, with photos and the names of the victims displayed on the walls.

88 That night, I can't get to sleep. In the dark, I'm imagining the flames as they ripped through the bunker. The fear. The cries. The silence.

89 It's hard to believe that not even a year ago there was a war. Baghdad has come back to life. The car horns. The weddings. Life has resumed.

90 I visit my paternal uncle Tarek. He lives in the Dora district, in the south of Baghdad. He's a widower with three daughters and a son.

91 Dora is a popular district. The houses are plainer than in Mansour and Amiriya. My uncle's has only a small living room with two bedrooms.

92 My cousin Ziad is sixteen. He's thin and dark-skinned. He asks a lot of questions about France. Especially about the girls there.

93 We wander around the neighborhood. Maybe there isn't any candy, but there is fresh fruit juice. My favorite is *batteekh*: melon.

94 Uncle Tarek is my father's older brother. He has blue eyes. A high forehead. When he smokes pensively, I see my father's face in the smoke.

95 My uncle is a man who was devastated by the loss of his wife. He takes care of four children on his own. The embargo has made it very hard. Ziad had to leave school.

96 Ziad works at the market, reselling things. He's mechanically inclined. A master of ingenuity at the young age of sixteen. He's impressive.

97 But Ziad has a heart defect. If he doesn't have an operation in the next year or so, his doctors say he won't live more than another fifteen years.

98 He needs a pacemaker. It's complicated in a country under embargo where you can't even get syringes and medications.

99 I come to the naive realization that I don't want for anything in France, that priorities aren't the same here. I feel privileged. And guilty.

100 Ziad introduces me to children in the neighborhood. I'm wearing a Nike T-shirt and Reebok Pumps. What happens next will mark me for life.

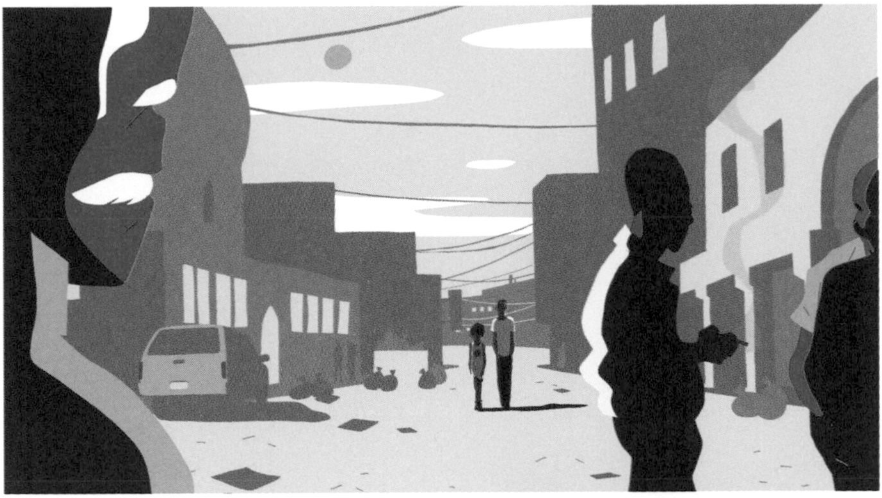
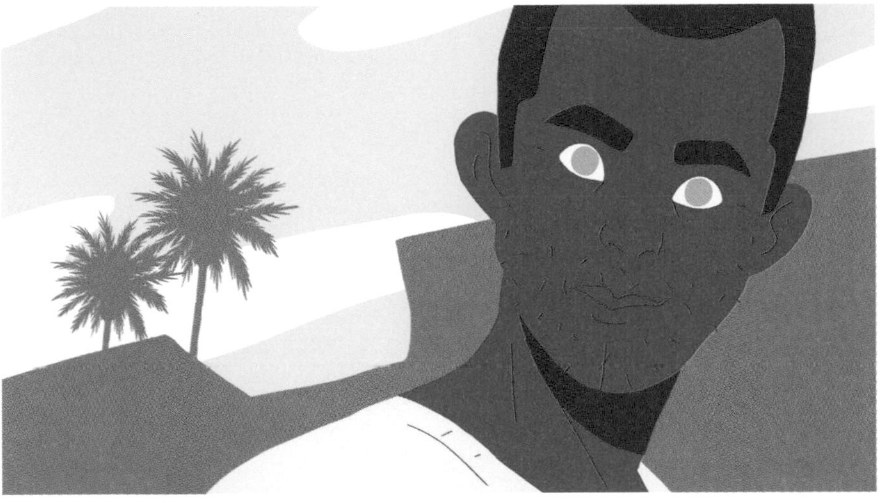
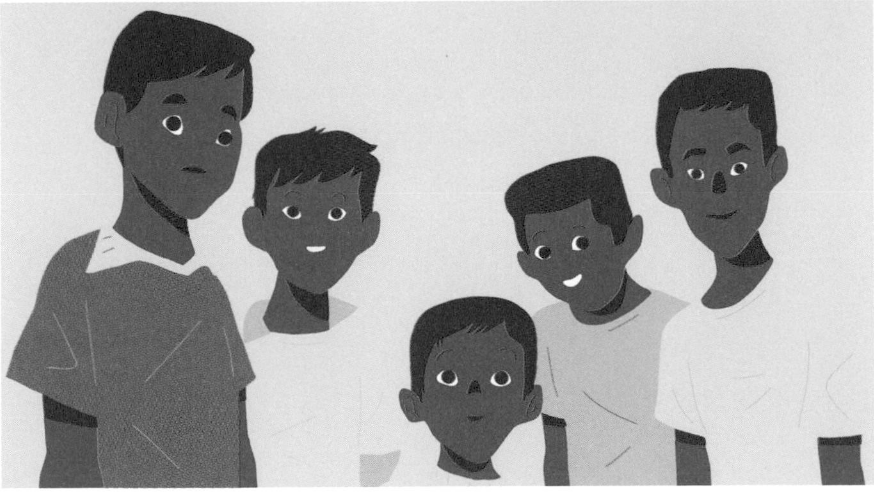

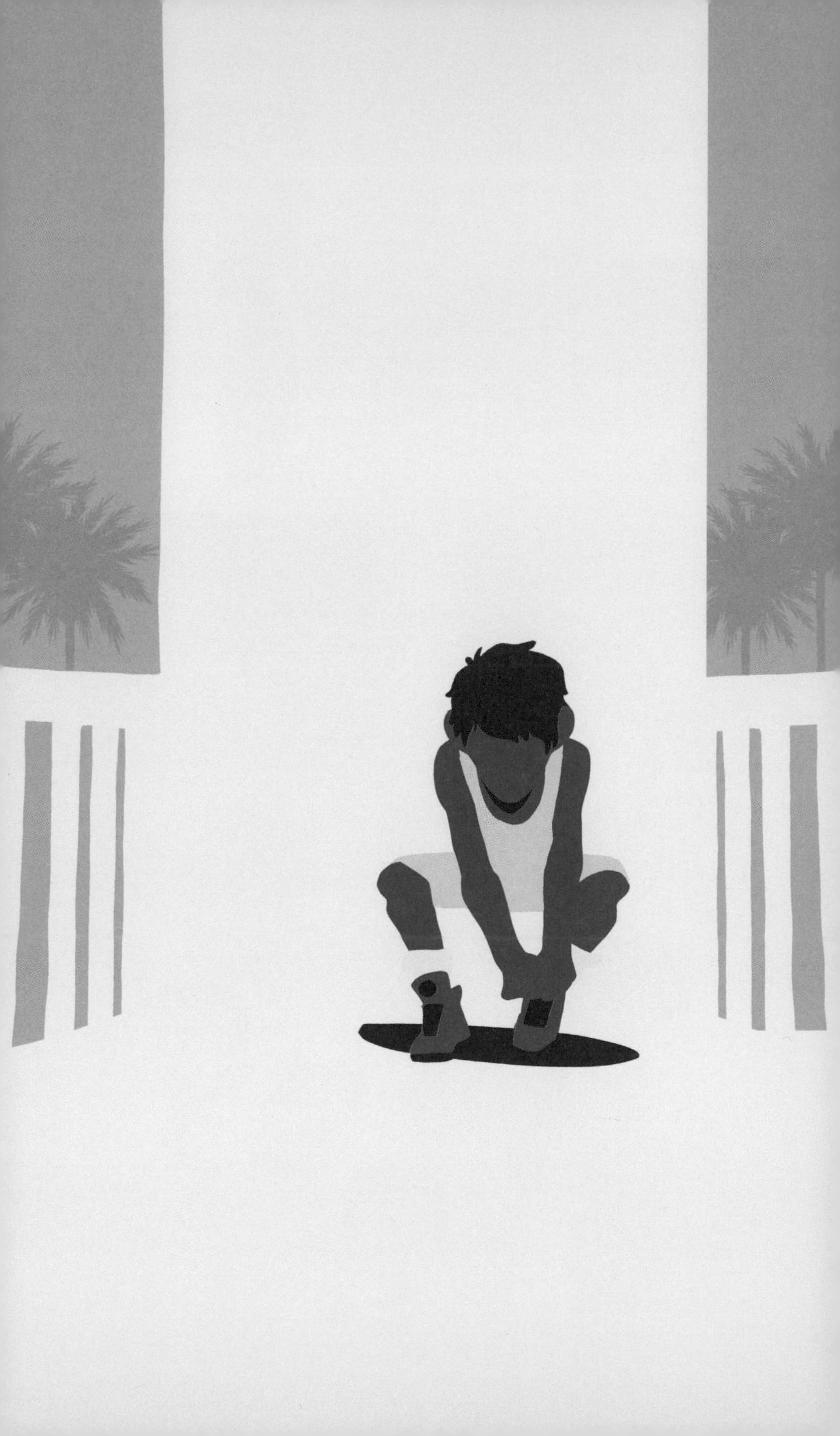

1992   **The summer ends in Baghdad. When I return to France, my friends tell me all about their vacations at the beach.**

101   Ziad tells his friends that I've come all the way from Paris. Curious, they draw near. About ten of them surround me with a friendly air.

102   They smile at me. They ask questions. I note how these kids—the same age as me—are fascinated by my Reebok Pumps and my Nike T-shirt.

103   I find it hard to bear because, with the embargo, sports-branded gear has become expensive and hard to get. And there I am with all of these children exactly my age who can only dream about it.

104   Even the older ones, like Ziad's friends, want to touch my Reeboks. The oldest holds out a set of keys. "My car for your shoes."

105   I think it's a joke. I'm twelve years old, I tell him. He insists. I refuse graciously. Ziad sees my discomfort. We politely take our leave.

106   Ziad and I say our goodbyes that day. I leave feeling guilty about my privileged childhood while they are deprived of the world.

107   My family in France is far from rich, but we live well. I start to believe that my father sent us here for that very reason.

108   I wait impatiently for my uncles from Fallujah to arrive. I've grown up. I want to prove it to them. We leave Baghdad in a decrepit Brasilia. I want to see my river again.

109   We arrive at my uncle Saad's in the evening. In the garden, the smoke from the barbecue is enticing. I'm hungry. The Iraqi kebabs are ready.

110   My uncle is limping more than he did in 1989. He needs a special procedure for his amputated foot. But he doesn't have a choice. It's impossible because of the embargo.

111 The landscape in Fallujah is in ruins. The war came through here, leaving in its wake more destitution, more dilapidation.

112 Here, the effects of the embargo are more evident. The town market shows the signs of this new poverty. Haggard faces, forced smiles.

113 In the Jolan family home, everyone is there. *Bibi* Samia, my uncles Ayad, Imad, Jamal, Riyad, and Mohamed, and my aunts Nahla and Souad.

114 *Bibi* Samia is just as lively as ever, in spite of her age. She talks over the others. She complains about the plight of the Iraqi soldiers.

115 My uncles were in the war. Jamal served with the air defense forces. The "fireworks" on TV, that was him.

116 Ayad lost three soldiers in his battalion. No medal this time. Not even what he needs to survive, given the decline of the dinar. He's angry.

117 His salary? 3,000 dinars. Doesn't really buy much. So he has to work. Most military officers are also taxi drivers.

Arab Socialist Ba'ath Party البعث العربي الاشتراكي Political party headquartered in Baghdad from 1968—2003 under the leadership of Saddam Hussein.

118 Anger is growing among the troops in Fallujah. Saddam Hussein is openly criticized, even at the local #BaathParty branch.

119 I have also noticed that there are more mosques now than in 1989. Religious fervor in Fallujah is stronger, more apparent.

120 Members of the Ba'ath Party, like my uncle Ayad, practice Islam openly. With the pressure of the blockade, the Ba'ath are quietly adapting.

121 My uncles, the children of *Bibi* Samia, aka "the boss," are the half brothers of my father, who lost his mother at the age of seven.

122 My father's mother had three boys and one girl before she died. My father was the youngest of the brothers. And, as a result, more vulnerable.

123 His half brothers were either not yet born or too young to understand. *Bibi* Samia made his life hard. He was bullied and humiliated on a daily basis.

British Occupation Iraq was a territory, rather than a colony, under British Administration from 1920 to 1932, after which the "Kingdom of Iraq" gained its independence.

124 My grandfather saw none of this—or didn't want to—disheartened as he was by his modest lifestyle following the #BritishOccupationofFallujah.

125 My uncles owe my father a debt of gratitude. When he became an adult and left to live in Baghdad, he would often send them money.

126 Instead of demoralizing his half brothers, he always treated them with kindness and respect.

127 Their eyes shine when they talk about my father. Arrested under Saddam for political reasons, he spent two months in Qassar al-Nihaya prison.

128 He was arrested for distributing anti-regime pamphlets opposing Saddam's increasingly authoritarian rule. When my father finally got out, no one was waiting for him.

129 In 1972, he went to France in pursuit of leftist revolutionary ideals. He wanted some distance before returning home.

130 His brothers and half brothers heard nothing of him until after the Iran–Iraq War in 1989, and they wondered, Would he ever return? He never did move back.

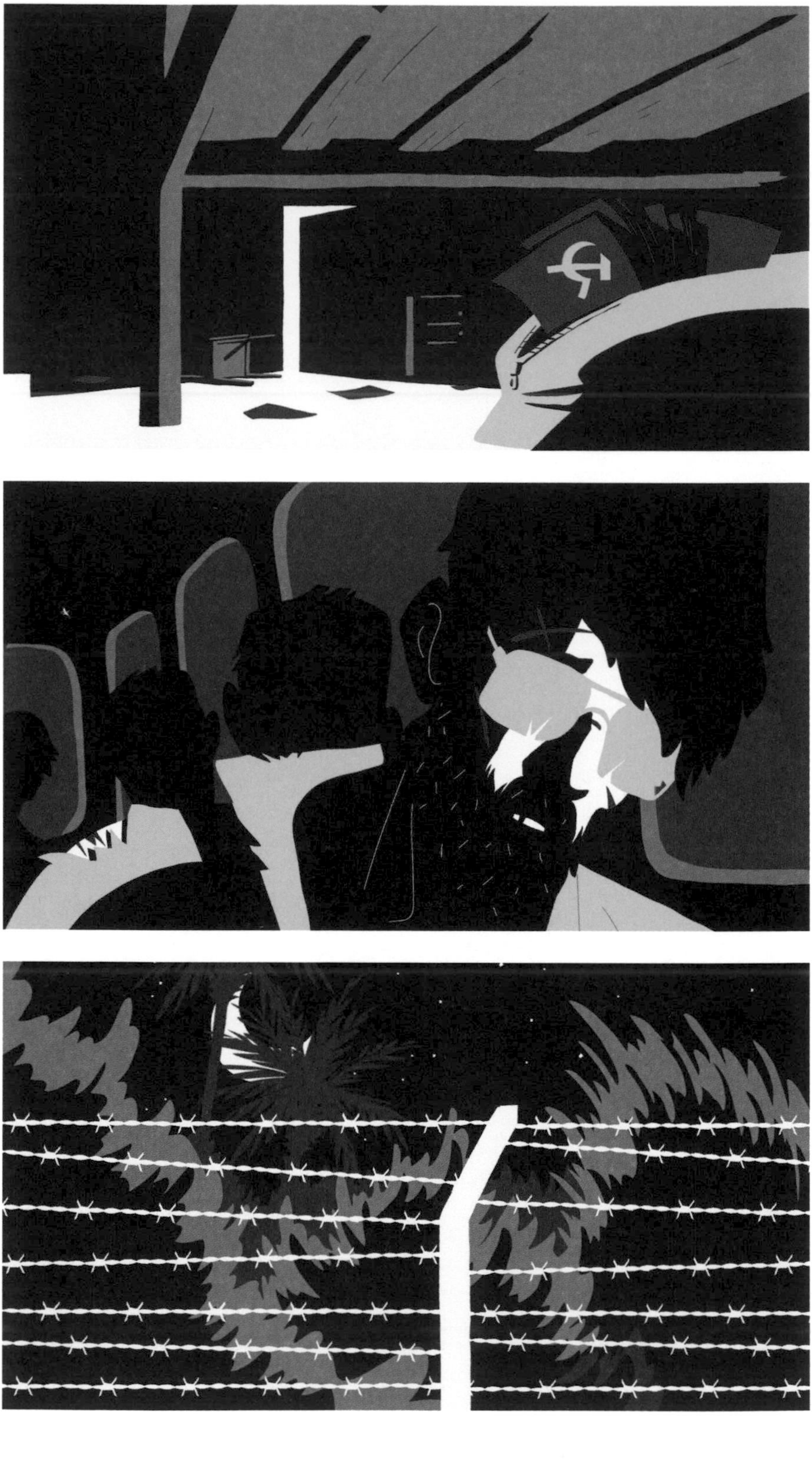

131 I meet the older brother of my father, Khaled, for the first time. He's a Sufi mystic. My father liked to say he "prayed morning, noon, and night."

132 I'm not familiar with Sufism. I was expecting to see a whirling dervish. Uncle Khaled is a #Naqsh-bandi. One of the earliest Sufi orders.

Naqshbandi
نقشبندية
The *tariqa Naqsh-bandi* is one of the four original orders of Sufism. It gets its name from Khwaja Shah Baha al-Din Naqshband, who is considered one of its masters rather than its founder. Abu Yaqub Yusuf al-Hamadani, born in 1048, and Abdul Khaliq Ghijduvani, born in 1103, est-blished the tenets of this branch of Sufism.

133 His beard is white, his gaze is deep, and his voice is soft. A peaceful aura surrounds his person. I like him already.

134 My father told me that Uncle Khaled has always been withdrawn. He is the imam of a mosque in Saqlawiyah, a village on the outskirts of Fallujah.

135 I learn that we descend from a line of imams, and that he is the last in line. He asks me questions about my life. His eyes are blue.

136 His son Walid greets me. He is tall and slim like my uncle Ayad. He will succeed Uncle Khaled as imam in the Saqlawiyah mosque.

137 The spirituality that reigns in this household is palpable. When my uncle Khaled walks down the stairs, he appears to be floating.

138 His charisma was his salvation a long time ago, according to my father. As a fervent believer, my uncle had refused to join the Ba'ath Party.

139 When he was called in to the local party office, the officers there threatened to kill him if he didn't join them. This happened a lot at the time.

140 Khaled told my father that his faith made him fearless. His response: "I will never be a member of a party of unbelievers."

141 Taken aback by such poise, the officers let him go without putting up a fight. After that, Uncle Khaled was never bothered or threatened again.

142 My mother is also a Fallujah native. Her father, who died before she was born, was a local dignitary, highly respected from Fallujah to Baghdad.

143 Giddu Khalaf was among the first to own a car in Fallujah. When he died, he left land and other assets to his wife and children.

144 In the early 1950s, my grandmother, now widowed, left Fallujah for Adhamiyah, an elegant historic district on Baghdad's right bank.

Tribes and other differences . . . The heightened fragmentation of Iraqi society at the local, regional, ethnic, and even tribal levels did a great disservice to the country's national identity, which has weakened but has not altogether disappeared. From 1920 to 1980, Iraq emerged as a secular state governed by political and/or militant groups who opted for an authoritarian and modernizing form of government, but one that owes its basic functioning to relationships based on allegiance and solidarity—what Ibn Khaldun calls *asabiyya*.

145 Part of the family remained in Fallujah. They have large homes and businesses, and they live much better than my paternal uncles.

146 My father's and mother's families don't associate. The difference in social status is significant, even though members of the same #tribe, whether from the city or the country, can cohabitate.

147 I'm too young to understand that this social "problem" will play a major role in Iraq after 2003. More on this to come.

148 In Fallujah, family solidarity plays an essential role in the fight against the embargo. To survive, the uncles on my father's side combine forces.

149 Each does what he can for the sake of the household. Life is hard, but life goes on, thanks to the different links in the family chain.

150 In 1992, in spite of the embargo, the country tries to rebuild from all the destruction caused by the war. The morale of Iraqis is strong.

151 Summer ends in Baghdad. When I return to France, my friends tell me all about their vacations at the beach.

152 It's 1995. One year ago, Saddam Hussein made an important political decision that authorized the return home of former dissidents.

153 Was my father's name now removed from the "list"? Uncle Jamal works in intelligence. He confirms that my father is now able to return home.

154 In early July 1995, the entire family travels to Jordan and then to Iraq. I wonder about my father. After 23 years of exile, how will he feel?

155 Will he remember the backstreets he roamed in Fallujah? The address of his apartment in Baghdad? The prison where he languished?

156 I feel a twinge of sadness. What if this was a trap? Very little information was coming out of Iraq at the moment. We land in Amman in the morning.

157 We get on the road that same evening. It's chaos at the Iraqi border because of an incident. A man tried to cross with a handgun.

158 Evidently, he hid it under a mountain of dates in the back of his truck. The atmosphere is tense. The *Mukhabarat* are gutting each vehicle.

159 They turn our 4×4 inside out during the search. While we wait, we're invited to go with one of the agents. We're coming from France, and that surprises them.

160 We take our seats. I cross my right ankle on top of my left knee. I don't realize that the sole of my shoe is pointed at the desk.

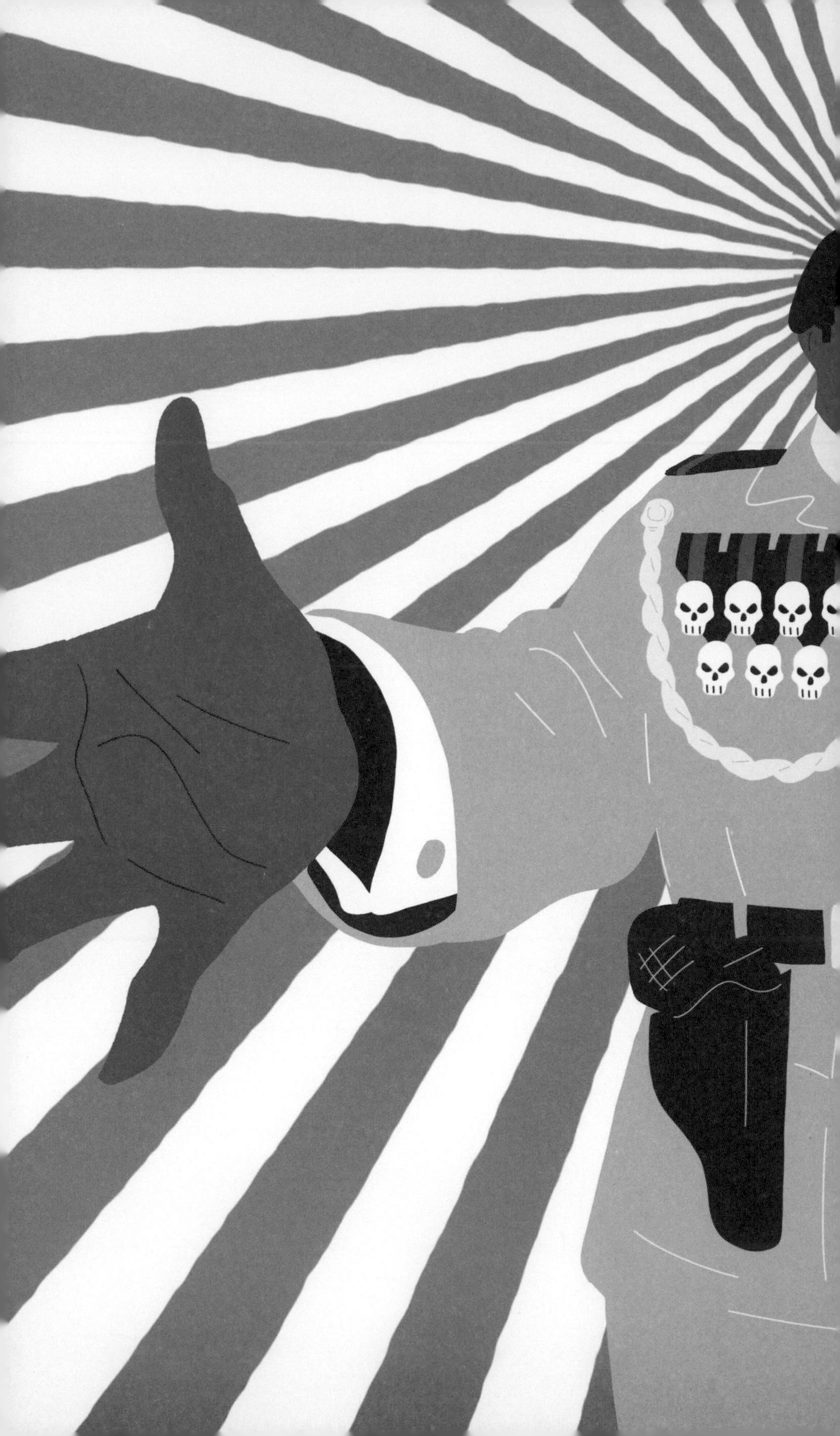

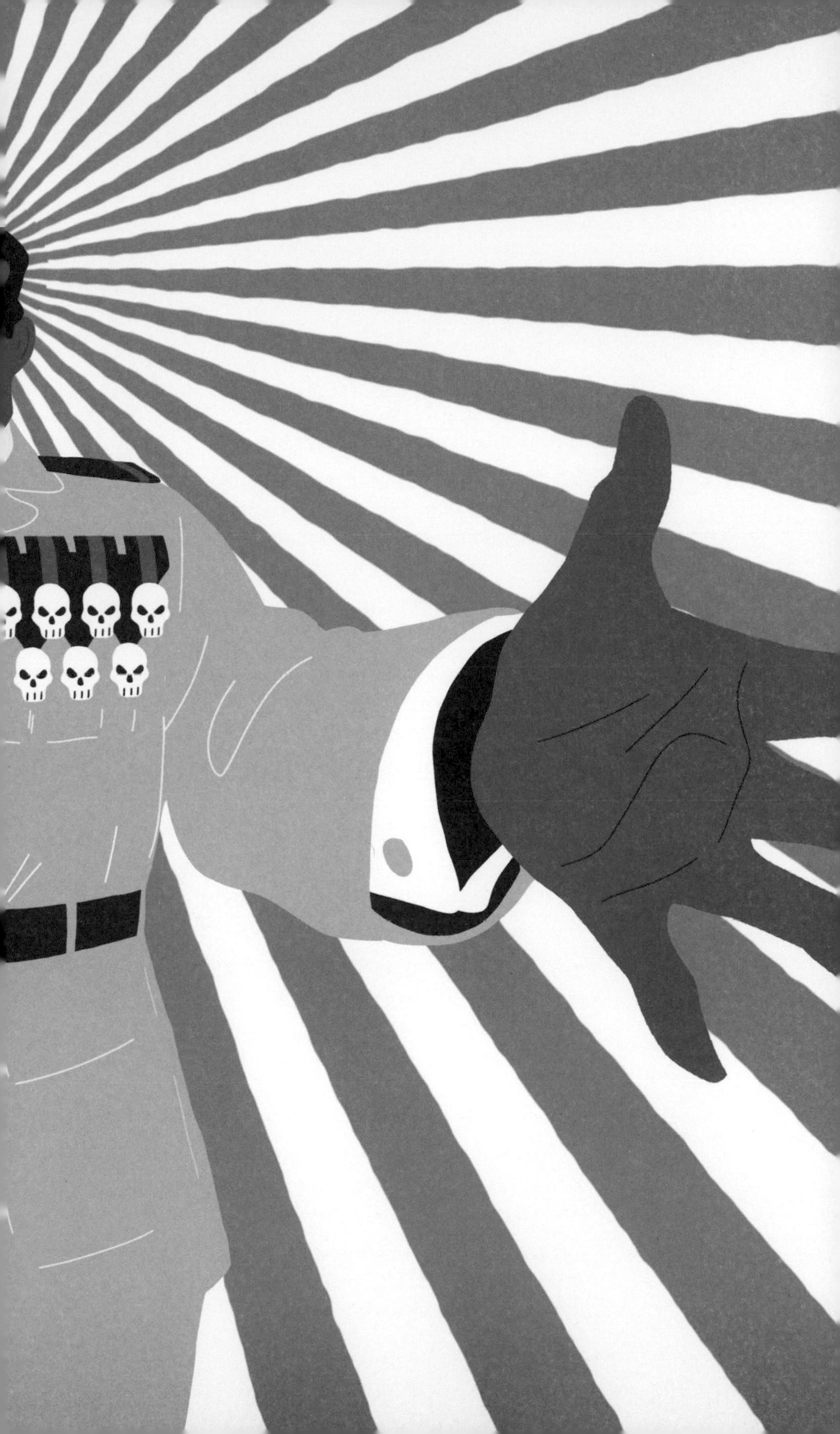

161   The *Mukhabarat* officer glares at me and starts shouting at me. He orders me to stand. The sole of my shoe pointed at his face makes him irate.

162   That's what offended this officer. My mother gets up: "He's only fifteen years old, he doesn't know!" The man calms down. My father looks at me.

163   I say nothing. I don't make eye contact with this little Hitler. I don't want us to lose valuable time. He's asking my father questions.

164   He lets us leave, but then we get stuck in traffic twelve hours from the Iraqi border. It's pure hell. 122°F outside. My sister loses it.

165   We arrive in Baghdad at dawn the next day after spending 24 hours in the car. There's an accident when we reach 14th July Street.

166   It's an ugly sight. One of the car's passengers is lying on the ground. The EMTs are there. Summer is starting on a morbid note—I don't like that.

167   We arrive at my aunt Enaam's house. I crash in one of the bedrooms. I haven't slept in 24 hours and am exhausted from the trip.

168   I wake up in the middle of the night to the sound of clinking dishes and silverware. People are here already. I hear my father's voice.

169   We are in the Yarmouk district, one of my favorite neighborhoods, along with al-Jadriya and Abu Nuwas. I take a walk with Mazen. He's my age.

170   Mazen is the son of my aunt Khamael. They live in the Amiriya district. His father was the governor of the Wasit province in the 1980s.

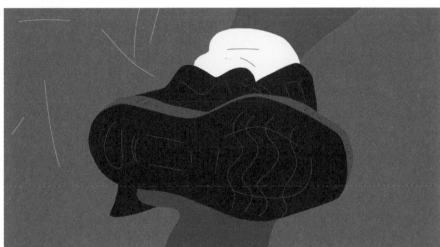

171 But he never did join the Ba'ath Party. Saddam wanted the western tribes to be under his command. Sometimes tribe came before party.

172 In 1989, one Iraqi dinar was worth $3.50 US. In 1995, after the devaluation, the US dollar is worth 2,000 dinars. It's an economic catastrophe.

173 Prices shot up, and the dinar fell. The few medications that were available went at exorbitant prices.

174 The list of prohibited items ranges from simple foodstuffs to almost all pharmaceutical products. Why?

175 At least 500,000 babies have died because of the embargo. Footage of this humanitarian disaster is exploited by the regime on Iraqi television.

176 The photos they show on air are horrible: sick babies, emaciated children in Baghdad and Basra after the 1991 bombings.

177 The Iraqis are demoralized. The embargo has become unbearable. The food shortages, the lack of healthcare—it's inhumane.

178 An embargo that was supposed to weaken the regime has only strengthened it. Publicly, people complain about what the embargo has done to their lives. Privately, they blame Saddam.

179 Maybe that's the point of this blockade. Weaken the people by depriving them of resources. Isolate them so they can one day be "liberated."

180 In 1995, the Iraqis no longer eat meat. Even at my rich aunt Soumaya's house in Mansour, there is no more meat. It's too expensive.

181 At dinner one day at Aunt Enaam's house, chicken thighs are on the table in the garden in honor of our visit. A scrawny cat meows at my feet.

182 I give him a piece of chicken. My cousin Raghad shrieks: "Iraqis are starving and *you're* feeding a cat?" Slap!

UN
The United Nations: An international organization formed in 1945 with the goal of maintaining peace and security throughout the world.

183 I have always wondered this: Why did the #UN prohibit the importation of basic staples to Iraq, such as flour and sugar?

184 Out on the Mansour sidewalk with Mazen, he tells me what he misses the most: chocolate and ice cream. Ice cream? It's forbidden, he says.

185 I laugh. But it's not a joke. In 1995, Saddam Hussein banned the sale of ice cream and sorbet in Iraq. The reason?

186 Priorities had to change when the heavy embargo made sugar such a scarce commodity. It couldn't be wasted. Extravagance was a thing of the past.

187 But for all banned substances—like drugs—there is a black market. That's the case for ice cream. This is also not a joke.

188 Our car pulls up in front of a house in Mansour. My cousin Taghreed tells me to come with her, and be quick about it. Mazen and my sister stay in the car.

189 We ring. A woman opens the door and silently looks us over. She leaves, then returns with two plastic containers. Money is exchanged.

190 Like two addicts, we leave with our stash. I feel like laughing. But in this summer heat, all I can think about is devouring the forbidden ice cream.

191   I open the container. In it are all the colors of the rainbow. The warm yellow looks like apricot. The four of us revel in the taste of the illicit.

192   I'm not exactly sure why, but for a split second I'm taken back six years to Iraq in 1989. The flavor of Baghdad. It stays with me.

193   In Fallujah, my father reunites with his brothers after a 23-year absence. *Bibi* Samia kisses him. Everyone is there. Uncle Imad weeps.

194   A large cloth is spread out on the ground and set with dishes. We have lunch. My father talks a lot. *Bibi* Samia, too. I try to imagine what they were like forty years ago.

195   Tea is served. My uncles gossip with my father like children. They tell him about the war. Who died, who is living, who fled.

196   Unlike my father's Fallujah of the 1950s, it is now a city in which the mosques stop time. At the hour of prayer, my uncles get up.

197   My father remains sitting. Two generations are side by side, each with a different story. Today, Fallujah is known as the "city of mosques."

198   Left to fend for itself, Fallujah sustained heavy damage during the Gulf War. In 1991, 1,360 civilians in the town marketplace were killed by British bombs.

199   Resentment toward Americans is already strong. With the embargo, the city is starting to become isolated from Baghdad.

200   It's developing a strong identity. My father reconnects with this city. No longer recognizing streets and houses, he gets lost. Everything has changed.

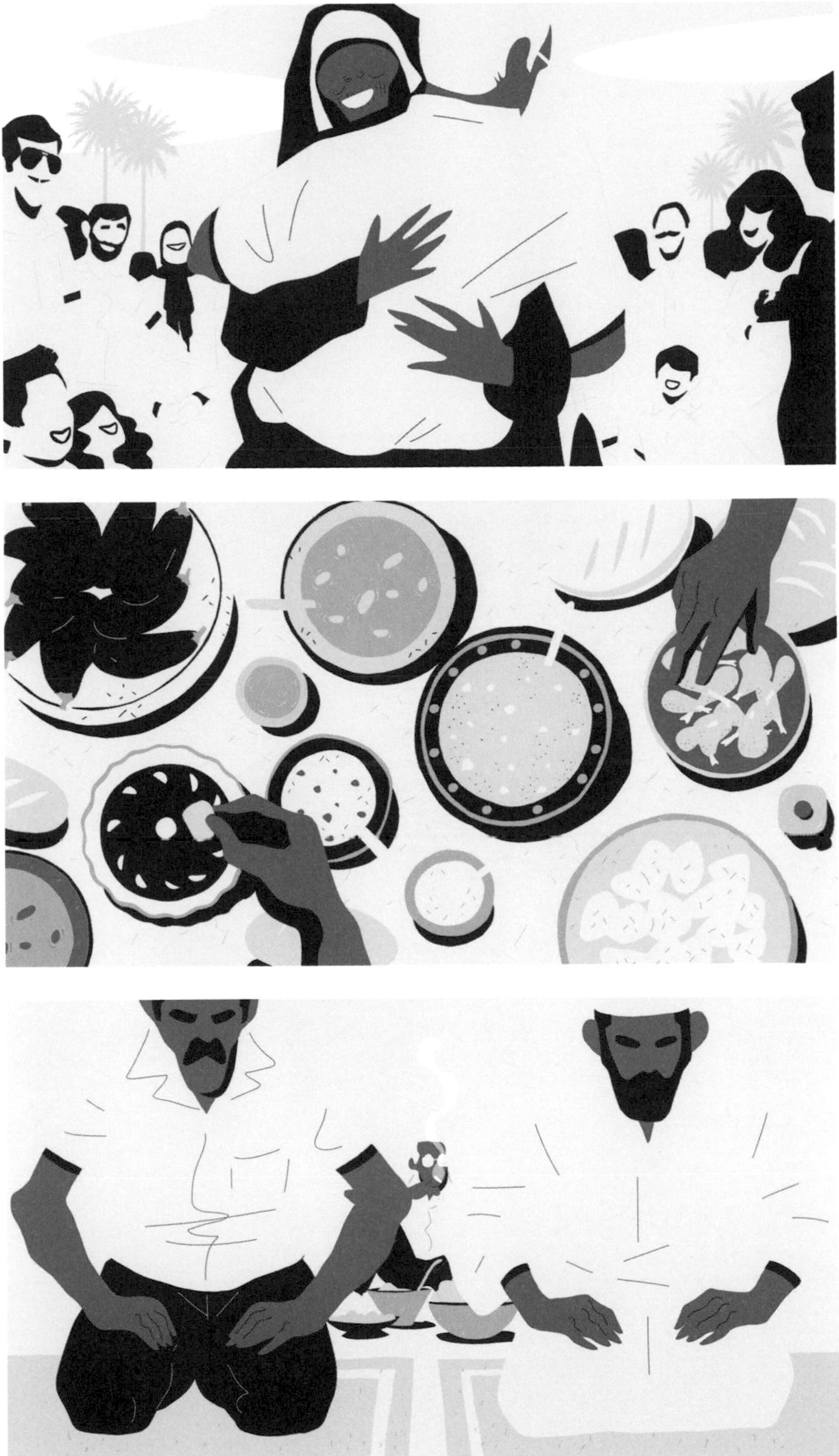

1995 If you really appreciate someone, you say "A khaliq ala rassi," or "I'll put you on my head."

201 We drive past his old elementary school. My father sold sesame bread—*simit*—in the street after school. He was six.

202 The Euphrates. A favorite pastime of young people, my father told me, was to bury watermelons at the bottom of the river. Then dig them out, once chilled, on a hot summer's evening.

203 We are going to visit my father's sister, Khaoula. She lives in very difficult conditions. Her son Ahmed is there.

204 A preadolescent in 1989, Ahmed is now 18. He's muscular and as resourceful as ever. He works at the market. He's the breadwinner of the family.

205 My uncles are there. The mood is festive. There's lots of joking. And laughter, too. I challenge Ahmed to arm wrestling. It was close, but in the end I lost.

Abaya
عباية
Traditional women's black overgarment that covers the body without covering the face, hands, or body. It can be worn with the *niqab*, a veil that covers all of the face except for the eyes.

206 My aunt Khaoula is short and wears the black #*abaya*. She rarely smiles. When she speaks to my father, her eyes look sad.

207 Auntie Khaoula, now a widow, was left with two sons without whom she would never get by. I don't understand why no one helps this abandoned woman.

208 Her home is hardly even a house. It's a room with unpainted bricks that serve as walls. The roof leaks sometimes. This breaks my heart.

209 There's hardly anything left to do in Fallujah. I no longer play with my uncles' handguns. And Uncle Imad's poems aren't as joyful.

210 *Bibi* Samia, "the boss," is still outspoken. She talks about my uncles' day-to-day activities. I gather she was a strict mother.

211　Raising sons for the military surely required an authoritarian approach. I can't help but think about everything my father has endured.

212　But in the end, fate was kind to my father. In spite of how difficult his life was in France, he was ultimately much better off there.

213　We go, for the first time, to visit my aunt Souad. She lives in a small, gray, cinderblock house in the al-Shuhada district.

214　Aunt Souad has blue eyes. Her children are younger than me. There's a music box in the room. A little dancer turns in pirouettes.

215　We sit around the table—the main activity when you're visiting with family. There are various Iraqi dishes. My favorite is *tashrib.*

216　It's a poor man's dish. Pieces of Arabic bread soaked in a red or white sauce with green onions. And meat, if possible.

217　It's hearty, inexpensive, and practical when you have ten at the table. I like this dish. Every country has its poor man's dish.

218　*Paella* in Spain, *koshari* in Egypt, *thieb* in Senegal. Quite often they're the most famous dish of a region. And the best.

219　With a stomach full of *taghrib,* I go for a walk with my cousins. It's 122°F outside. Someone starts to kick around a soccer ball. I sit down. I'd rather play basketball.

220　My uncle Riyad picks me up in his car. He talks with his hands. In two years, he'll be able to leave the army and go back to university.

221   He takes me to a traditional café. They're playing dominos and *tawli*—backgammon. Tea is poured, and smoke from cigarettes spirals upward.

222   At the time, some things might be hard to get in Fallujah, but you can usually get what you want. There are CD-ROMs, cigarettes, pool tables. People dream of happy tomorrows.

223   It seems like I'm the only one who cares much about Fallujah. It's an insignificant town at the time. A point of passage to Baghdad.

224   I walk downtown with my father. He tells me that Fallujah has built a strong identity, both in connection with and separate from Baghdad.

225   *With* Baghdad, because Fallujis wanted to study and even live in the capital. Baghdad holds a lot of sway over the city of mosques.

226   *Separate from* Baghdad, because Fallujah, too, has a distinctive history. In 1920, the Iraqi revolt against the British intensified in Fallujah.

227   It was the assassination of an officer of His Majesty the King in British-occupied Iraq that helped provoke the revolution.

228   The city of Fallujah was to become the heroine in songs that glorified the Revolution of 1920. Fallujah signifies revolt. And national pride.

229   Sunni tribes helped build the strong identity of this city along the Euphrates. We stop on the banks of the river.

230   My father learned how to swim in the Euphrates and practically drowned doing so. He tells me that there are whirlpools in places.

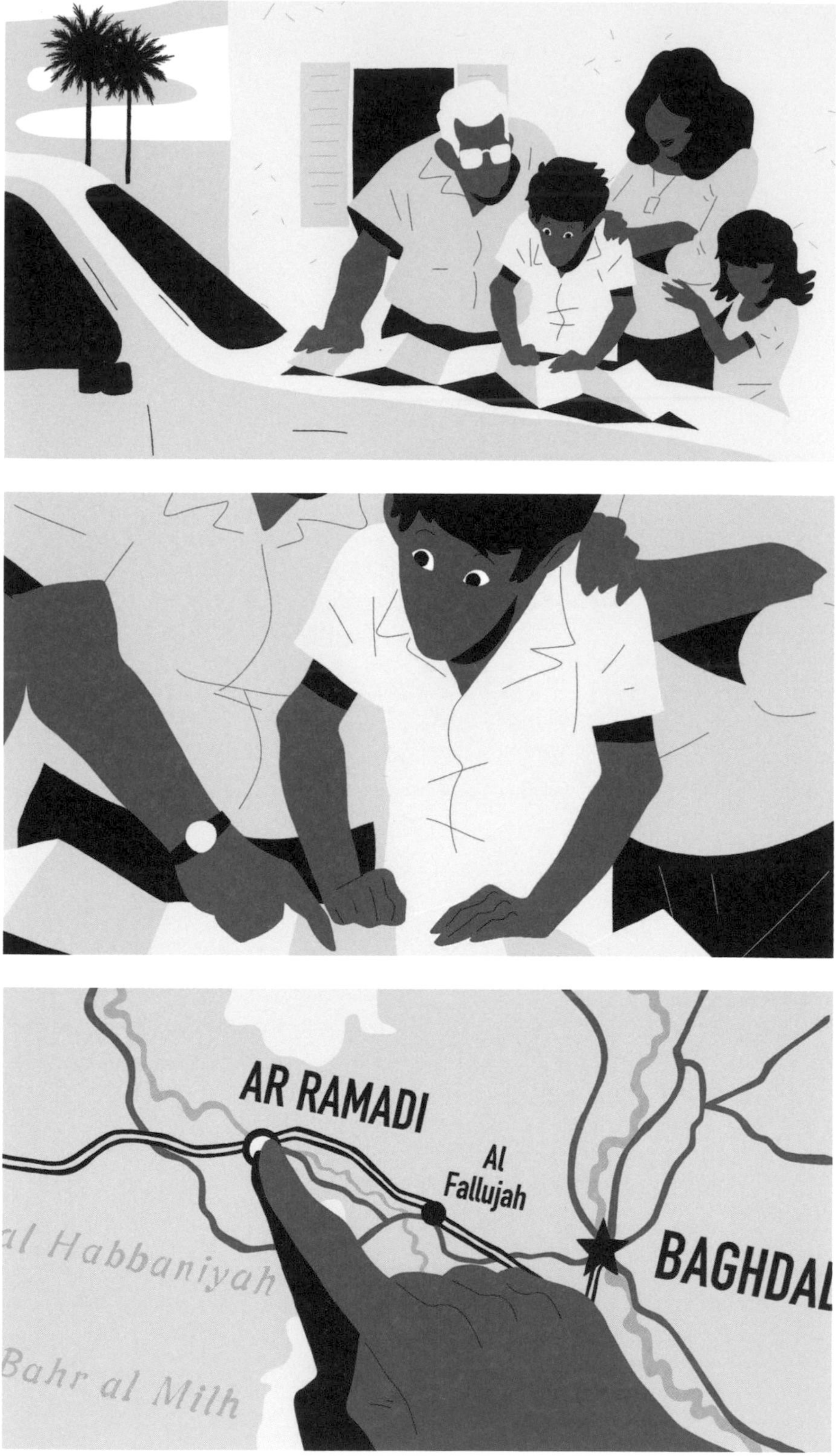
AR RAMADI
Al Fallujah
BAGHDA
al Habbaniyah
Bahr al Milh

231 The water is turquoise. Children are jumping off the green bridge and into the river. We leave here to go spend one last night in Fallujah. It will soon be time to go.

232 Tomorrow we'll go to Ramadi to visit my maternal cousin Auday. Ramadi is the largest city in al-Anbar, 130 km west of Baghdad.

233 Ramadi is a more imposing city than Fallujah. Downtown is bustling. The houses are luxurious. It's surrounded by the desert.

234 We visit my aunt Makarem. She's the widow of my maternal uncle Adel, a pilot in the Iraqi Air Force. She has two children, May and Auday.

235 May is the older of the two. She smiles all the time and loves to hug us, my sister and me. Auday is wearing the French team's jersey.

236 I've never met a bigger fan of the French soccer team. He knows their history by heart. He adores Platini.

237 At his request, I brought him some *Onze Mondial* soccer magazines. It's something I do for him every year. You can't get them here.

238 If I give him the date of a match for the French team in 1960, say, Auday can tell me, within a minute, who scored.

239 His knowledge and passion are the envy of all his friends in Ramadi. His cousin Hussein roots for Brazil. They rag on each other. I laugh.

240 If Auday is such a fan of team *bleu-blanc-rouge*, it's because he traveled to France in '82, to visit us in Poitiers. I was two.

241 He watched the 1982 World Cup, in Spain that year, on TV. Platini's France lost the third-place play-off. But Auday was starstruck.

242 He returned home with a love for France in his veins, Panini stickers, and a jersey. He still has these today in Ramadi.

243 It's in Ramadi that I discover the different tribes of al-Anbar. Auday is a "Jumaili," which originated in Garma, near Fallujah.

244 Tribes can play an important role in society, and sometimes even in the courts. Legal disputes are often resolved within and by tribes.

245 So much so that Saddam became wary, Auday told me. The *rais* even had the *nisba*, or tribal name, removed from identification cards.

246 The conflict between national citizenship and tribal affiliation is not new in Iraq. When the state is weak, the tribe is strong. And vice versa.

247 In spite of all that, Saddam tries to form an alliance with the tribes during the embargo. He gives them arms and assigns them the role of local protectors.

248 Auday never knew his father, my uncle Adel. In 1973, Adel died in the cockpit of his MIG-21 over Lake Habbaniyah, between Fallujah and Ramadi.

249 Auday was only one. His mother, Makerem, never remarried. His family gave Uncle Adel the nickname "the lion" because of his charisma.

Ahmed Hassan al-Bakr
أحمد حسن البكر
President of the Republic of Iraq from 1968 to 1979.

250 In 1969, he was sent to the USSR by the #alBakr regime, to the city of Krasnodar, where he was trained as a fighter pilot. The MIG-21 would ultimately become his coffin.

251 Some spoke of sabotage. Uncle Adel was close to al-Bakr, not to Saddam. And Auday can't request an investigation. It's too dangerous.

252 When I saw a photo of Uncle Adel in uniform wearing a Breitling on his left wrist and a confident expression on his face, I knew I was looking at a hero.

253 In Ramadi, I learn that *Dulaim* is the name of the iconic tribe in al-Anbar, which is the largest province in Iraq.

254 To be a Dulaimi is to be generous. Generous with one's words, with one's opinions, with how one welcomes others, and especially with the kinds of dishes one offers to guests.

255 Everywhere we go in Ramadi, whether visiting friends or family, we are greeted like kings. Even more so than in Baghdad and Basra.

256 In taxis, for example, the driver always offers a cigarette to passengers. Exaggerated gestures of politeness.

257 If you want to show appreciation for someone, you say "A khalik ala rassi," or "I'll put you on my head." It means going out of your way to help someone else.

258 I make a note of all these expressions. If someone openly admires my wristwatch, I must respond with *gidamek*—it's yours.

259 Supposedly, the person you say that to will always decline if you offer them your watch. It's simply a polite gesture, albeit a little over the top.

260 In Ramadi, showing generosity is sometimes a competitive sport. The tribe that slaughters the most sheep for its guests, for example. . . .

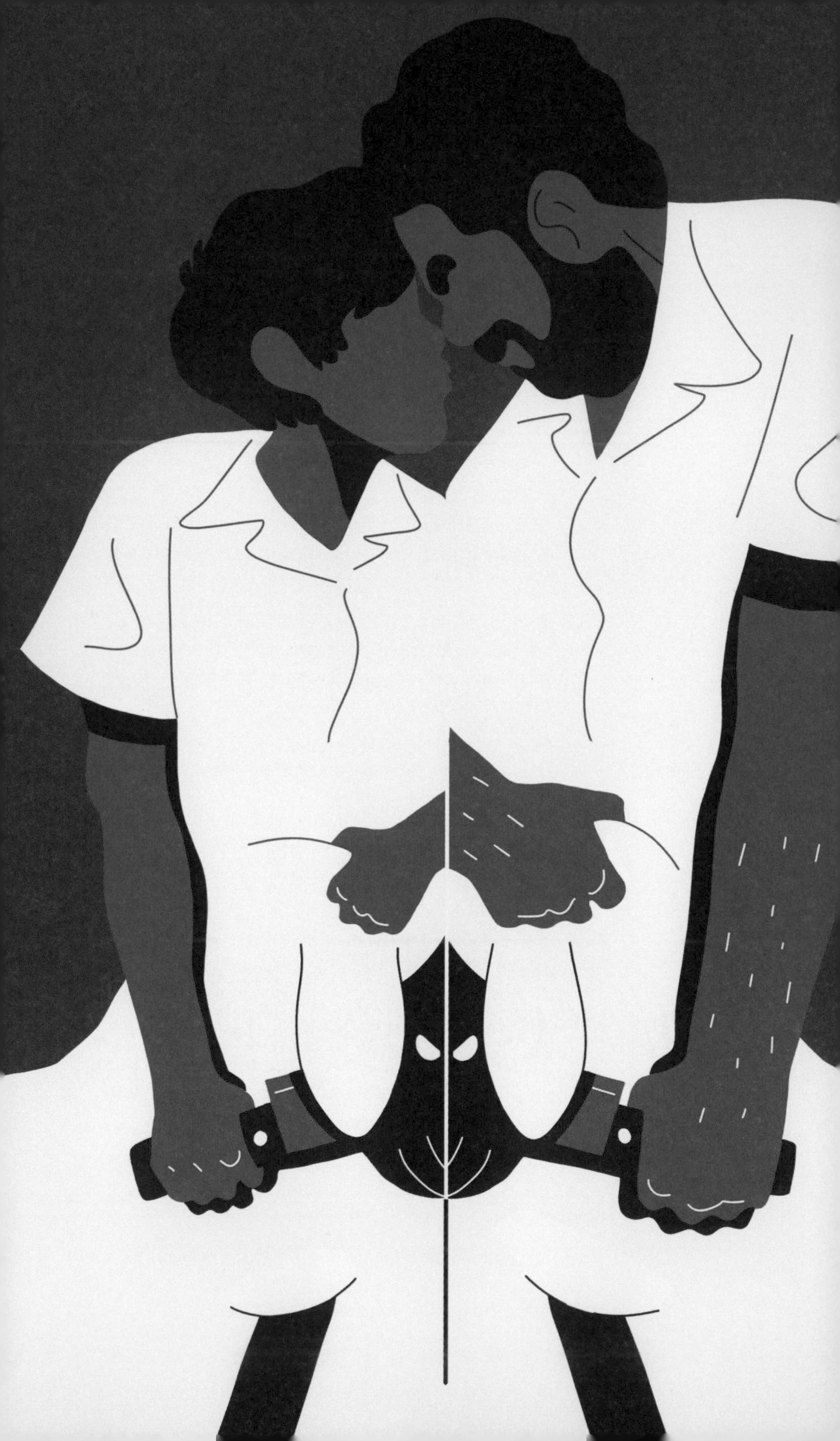

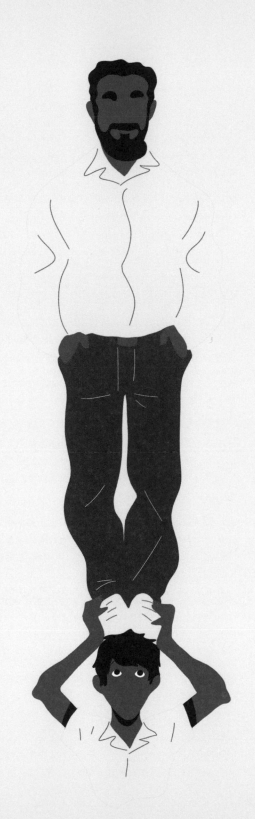

261 We go to a downtown restaurant with Auday. There's shouting inside. A fight? Yes, but over the matter of who will pay the check.

262 Auday tells me that guns are sometimes brandished if a sheik's honor is insulted because he wasn't allowed to pay the bill. Dangerous theater.

Nadi al-Seid Hunting Club
Private club in the Mansour district of Baghdad where members of the Iraqi elite socialize.

263 Back in Baghdad. My father has important meetings. I spend a week with Mazen. We play basketball at the #NadiAlSeid—the hunting club.

264 People play sports there during the day. At night, it's a hot spot for the elite. The highest tower in Baghdad is there—the *burj Saddam*: 205 meters.

265 At the very top there's a panoramic restaurant with a breathtaking view. They say that Saddam's son, Auday, goes there often.

266 You eat well in this restaurant. It's one of the few places of privilege in the embargoed city of Baghdad. Meanwhile, down below, people are suffering. The disparity is striking.

267 On the one hand, there are people who are hurting, and on the other, there's this little bubble of privilege. Some of my family in Mansour on my mother's side are part of this group.

268 Uncle Aziz works as a representative for L'Oréal in Iraq. In 1995, the embargo blocked the import of products. So he makes his shampoos here.

269 My cousin Taghreed is the factory's nose. She smells all the new shampoos. Problem: they smell good, but the scent doesn't last.

270 They're missing an important ingredient that can't be legally imported into Iraq: "too dangerous." Like pencils, which are forbidden because the graphite can be used to make weapons.

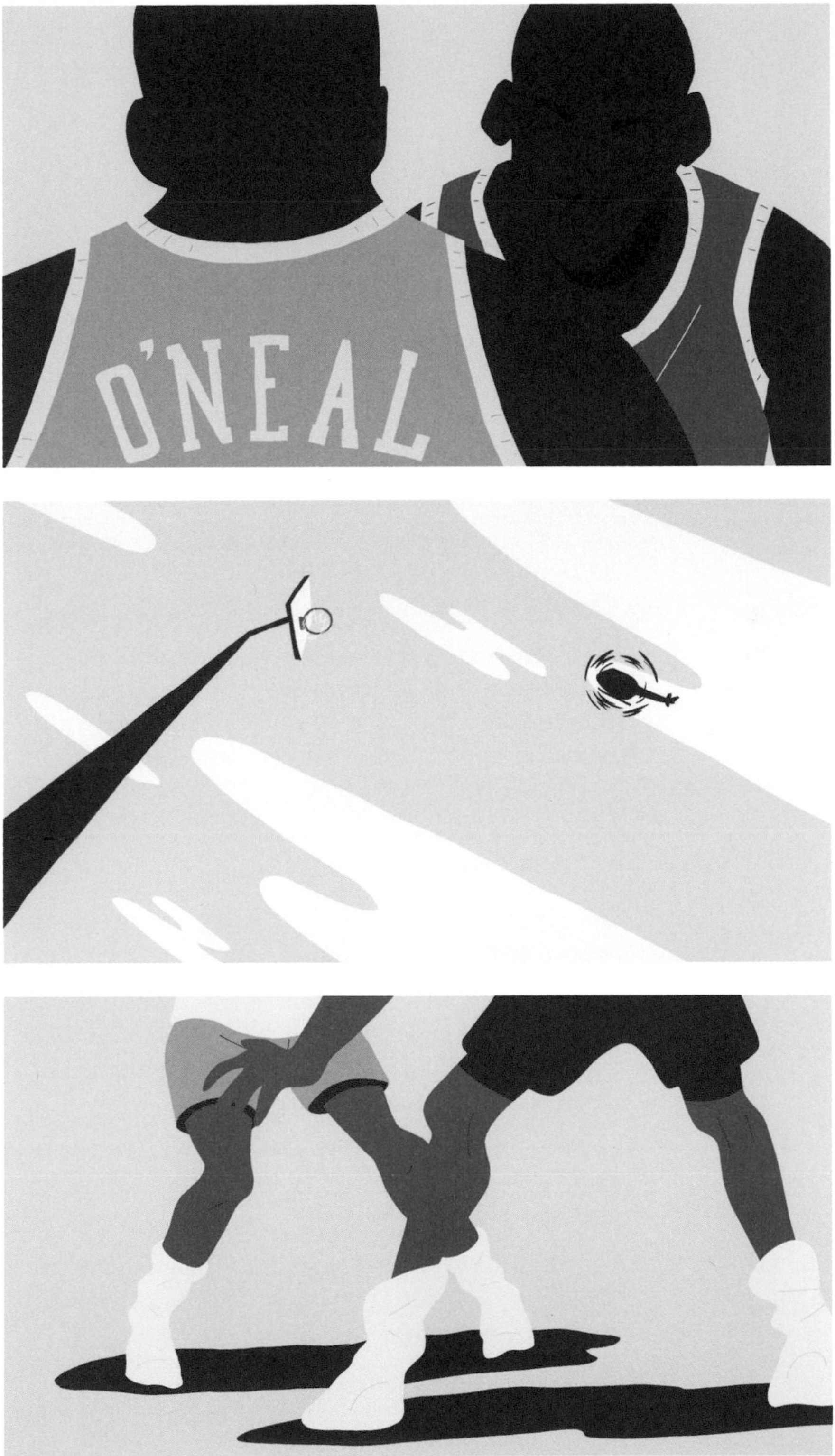
O’NEAL

271 It's very hot outside. While everyone is taking a nap, Mazen and I are hanging out in the living room. We find a pack of Winston cigarettes.

272 It belongs to my father. We each grab a smoke. The first draw makes me horribly nauseous. But Mazen keeps puffing. He'll be a smoker.

273 As summer begins in Baghdad in 1995, Mazen and I are on the basketball court. This is the year the Chicago Bulls lost to the Orlando Magic.

274 I want to avenge the Bulls. Two players show up. A two on two gets underway. I'm playing against the Orlando Magic, and, like the Bulls, I lose. By six points.

275 After two hours in the sun, my head is pounding blood like a heart. I'm hot. Mazen and I go back to the house in Mansour.

276 We relax in one of the bedrooms. The ceiling fan is on, thanks to a generator that kicks on when the electricity goes out.

277 Mazen proposes a silly contest: The one who touches the ceiling with his fist wins. He jumps— nothing. I jump—and smack.

278 One of the blades of the ceiling fan hits me in the head. I meet his challenge, but I fall back down with hair in my hands.

279 My scalp is slashed open. More blood than I've ever seen is streaming down my face. Mazen runs to get help. Discreetly.

280 He returns with the discretion of Iraqis: eight people, screaming. Taghreed is a pharmacist, and she puts a bandage on the wound.

281   Saad starts the BMW. He speeds at 160 kph on the highway from Mansour to Yarmouk. We reach our destination. I'm about to see what a hospital is like under the embargo.

282   It's chaos inside the Yarmouk hospital. Everything is dirty. There's screaming. Women in black. Crying. And the smell.

283   The corridor is overflowing. Women dressed in black are sitting on the ground. They have settled in here and are weeping. It feels like a funeral home.

284   I have to step over pools of blood and vomit. We get to a room. One of the doctors is stitching up a woman.

285   Then it's my turn. The doctor looks me over. I'm going to need about five stitches. But without anesthetic. "Too expensive," he explains.

286   My cousin Saad steps into the conversation. He insists on my having anesthesia. A negotiation. In the end, I will be anesthetized.

287   After two pokes, the doctor begins sewing. Mazen watches out of the corner of his eye. I want only one thing: to get out of this run-down hospital.

288   The doctor is done. Saad gives him a wad of bills. I realize it's for the anesthesia. 100,000 dinars, to be exact.

289   I'm stunned by what just happened. The doctor just made a deal with the little bit of anesthesia he had left. 100,000 dinars' worth. . . .

290   A fortune for anesthesia. I think about others who'll need similar treatment but don't have the means. Stitched up with no thing for the pain.

291 There's a ridiculous bandage around my face. We leave the hospital. I hate all of this. I just want to go home and sleep.

292 In 1995, my little accident taught me about two things: the state of Iraqi hospitals and the inequities of healthcare under the embargo.

293 I have a lump in my throat. The shrieking in the Yarmouk hospital haunts me. Where is my country as I knew it in 1989? Was it a mirage?

294 I want to have the last word, but I fall into a deep sleep under the ceiling fan. I wake up in the middle of the night, covered in sweat. The electricity was out again.

295 Iraq in 1995, that very dark year of the embargo, is a heavy burden on my adolescent shoulders. It makes me think. I don't want to play basketball anymore.

296 I have to keep my ridiculous bandage on for two weeks. I spend my days playing cards with my cousins Taghreed and Raghad.

297 I observe all the guests who come for dinner each night. Their profiles. Their way of speaking. Their clothes. I become an anthropologist.

298 There are the "Arabs" who come in from the rural areas. There are the mafia types with big bellies who play cards while drinking whiskey.

299 There are the women who chatter among themselves, drinking up the gossip like it's tea: *He said this, she said that.* Whispers, laughs.

300 I learn to listen without being noticed. Innocence is my alibi. My ears are like tools. I needed something to do.

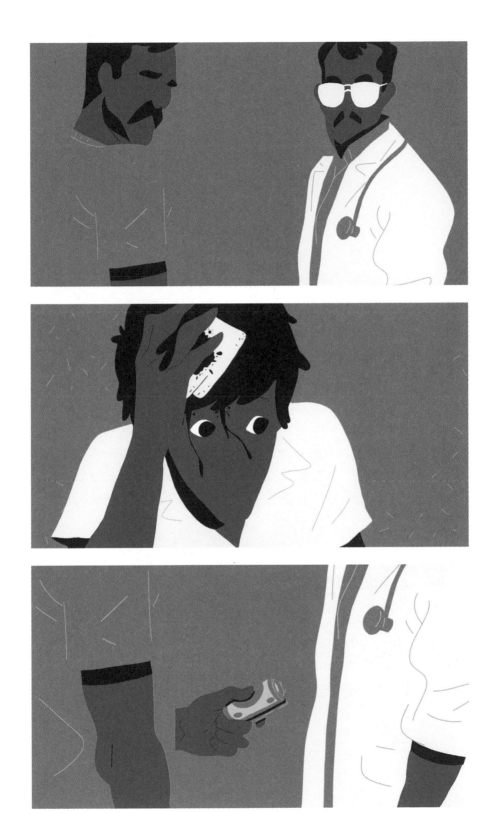

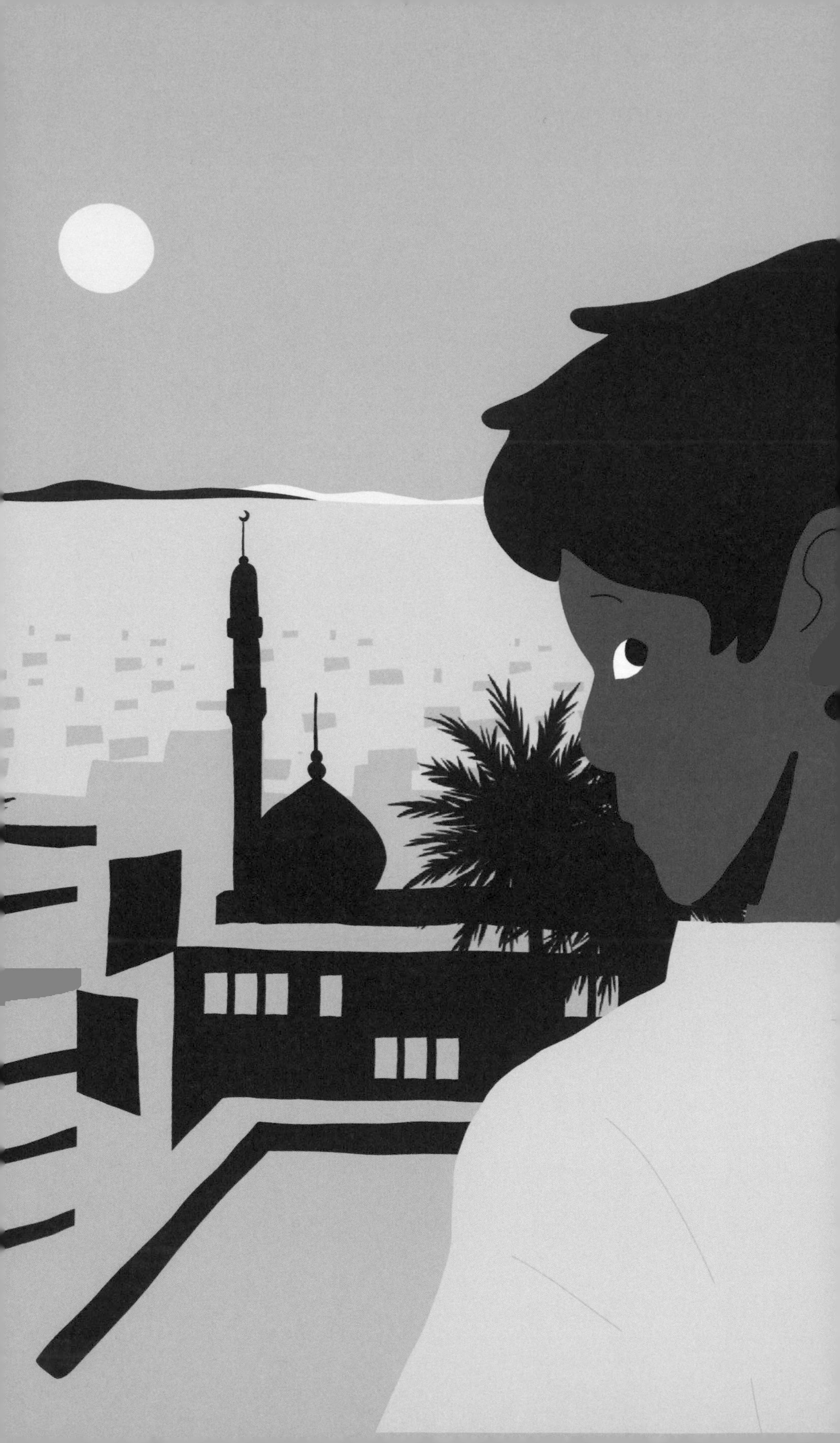

1995 A question from the disillusioned teenager I've become: Why was I born in France instead of Iraq?

301 I was starting to think that I wanted to leave Iraq. I didn't like this summer where too many things were blowing up in my face. Like the embargo.

302 This evening it's not gossip that stirs up the family but a man on the run. Hussein Kamel, the *rais*'s son-in-law, has defected to Jordan.

303 The head of Iraq's military industry has fled with his family and sensitive documents. He wants to speak to the West. He wants to betray his country. Saddam closes the borders.

304 Footage of the incident is the lead story on the television news. Hussein Kamel, his wife and children, and his brother Saddam Kamel flee Iraq by helicopter.

IAEA
International
Atomic Energy
Agency

305 Hussein Kamel leaves with classified documents about the Iraqi weapons program. He hands it all over to #IAEA and #UNSCOM.

UNSCOM
United Nations Spe-
cial Commission

306 It's an unbelievable disgrace for Saddam's regime. Jordan grants asylum to the defectors, and negotiations with the #CIA get underway.

CIA
US Central Intelli-
gence Agency

307 With the Iraqi borders now closed, we're stuck here until there's a new order from the government. My sister explodes with joy. My heart aches.

308 Are we going to remain stuck in Iraq under the embargo, never to see France again? It felt sickeningly oppressive.

309 At a certain point, Hussein Kamel's documents are no longer of use to the CIA. The UN and the Americans toss him aside scornfully.

310 The borders reopen. But Hussein Kamel's defection has led to paranoia within the regime. The *Mukhabarat* are nervous. Everyone is whispering.

311 Summer ends on a dystopian note. Everyone is surveilling everyone else. The regime tightens its hold. The Iraqis are feeling the pain.

312 In '96, Hussein Kamel returns to Iraq. Saddam supposedly forgives him for defecting. But he will be killed by his own clan. In the name of honor.

313 Later that same year, the US ambassador to the UN, Madeleine Albright, will say unapologetically that the death of 500,000 Iraqi children was worth it.

314 My eyes were bright with hope in 1989. Now in 1995, my heart aches with pain. I leave Iraq to its litany of miseries. We return to France.

315 A question from the disillusioned teenager I've become: Why was I born in France instead of Iraq? What would have become of me there?

316 My father's exile had spared my sister and me from having to live through the war with Iran and later the Gulf War and the injustice of the embargo.

317 They say you must never forget where you come from. I don't, but I have a hard time with it. I read somewhere that this is called "imposter syndrome."

318 I should have been born in Fallujah. The hypocrisy is that I was born in Paris. I should have had to live with bombs and shortages. I live in peace.

319 I'm feeling like I'm out of place. Fake. Culpable. I want to forget, but the time I spent in the land of my roots stays with me.

320 We're among the limited number of Iraqis who knew what our country was like prior to 2003. My sister and I learned Arabic in Iraq. An incredible advantage.

321 When I tell stories about Iraq to my friends, I keep to myself my indescribable sadness. Like what it feels like to witness the downfall of Mesopotamia.

322 Evenings, I write letters to my family in Baghdad and Fallujah. Send them to Iraq? The embargo won't let me.

323 I hear my father say to my mother that we won't go back home next year. Nor the year after. Will I ever breathe the air of Iraq again?

324 Seven years have passed. It's 2002. Iraq is still standing. In spite of the embargo, the situation there is a lot better than in 1995.

Oil-for-Food Program
A program to address the humanitarian needs of the Iraqi people after the Iraq–Kuwait conflict (also called the "Second Persian Gulf War," the first being the Iran–Iraq War). It was instituted to alleviate the protracted suffering of the Iraqi people caused by the UN-imposed economic sanctions following Iraq's invasion of Kuwait in 1990.

325 This is no doubt thanks to one of the most obscene institutional scams the world has ever known—the #OilForFoodProgram.

326 On the backs of the Iraqi people, Saddam's regime has been making trade deals with 2,200 companies by lowering the price of oil by 50 euro cents a barrel. He's been doing this since 1996.

327 Companies buy the oil at 50 cents under value and then return 25 cents per barrel to Baghdad. That's two billion dollars just thrown away. The UN knows this.

328 The UN is even complicit. Kofi Annan's son is involved, for instance. That's when I lost all hope in the UN.

329 Iraq also traffics in contraband oil by overloading tankers. A surplus the Iraqis don't see a drop of.

330 By way of this scandal, Iraq hopes that the "friends" they have in France and Russia will pressure the UN to lift the embargo. What a load of crap.

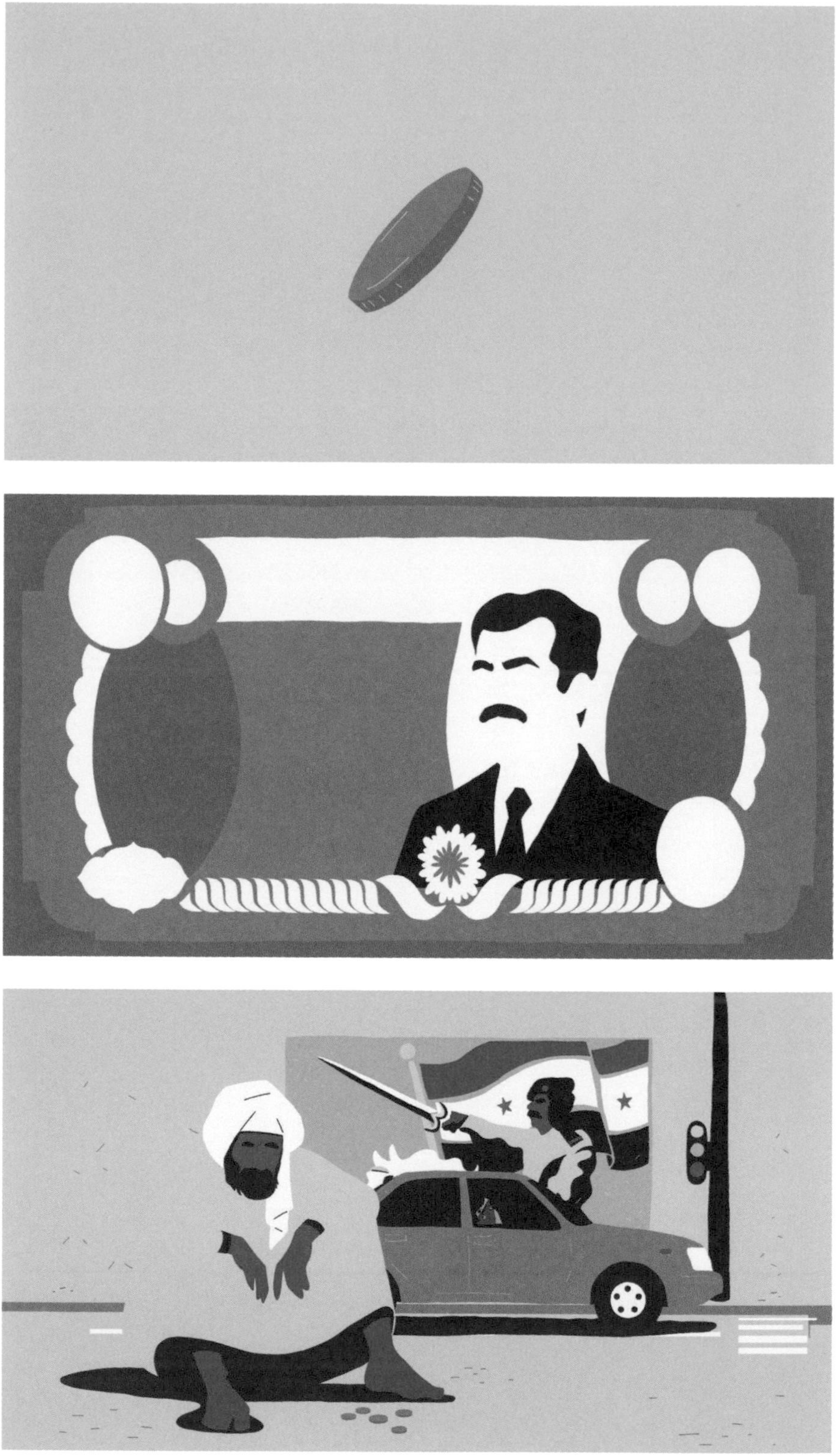

Charles Pasqua
(April 18, 1927–
June 29, 2015)
French politician,
Interior Minister
from 1986 to 1988
and from 1993 to
1995.

331 The names of #Pasqua and other French figures are mentioned. I think of my family and friends in Iraq. It's sickening.

332 This shocking scandal certainly makes the front page of the papers for a while. But no one is punished. Kofi Annan remains in his position.

333 Of all the tragedies that have befallen Iraq, it's this one that makes me want to tell Iraq's story. To make this my profession. I look into journalism schools.

334 In 2002, I get news from Mazen, the cousin who helped me after my accident in Baghdad in 1995. He was with me in the Yarmouk hospital.

335 Mazen is in medical school. He watched the doctor sew up my scalp after my accident with the fan blade. Mazen says he found his calling that day.

336 In Fallujah, *Bibi* Samia is doing well and still talking a lot. My uncle Imad continues his work as an administrative writer in the courthouse downtown.

337 The others are working. Jamal wants to be a professor. Riyad teaches history. Saad is retired. Mohamed is a mechanical engineer.

338 My first cousins once removed have grown up. It's hard to count everyone. I make a list of all their names. Between Baghdad and Fallujah, there are about one hundred of them.

339 My cousin Lubna from Yarmouk is married to an Iraqi abroad. She now lives in the United States. In Dallas, Texas, the stomping grounds of the Bush family.

340 In spite of the embargo, the news about Iraq is not so bad. There is some semblance of normal existence in 2002. That dark year of 1995 is in the past.

341 But the Iraqis are tired. The wars and the 12-year blockade have wrapped them up in a Teflon bubble.

342 Very few have internet access or cell phones. Satellite dishes are officially prohibited, even though the regime looks the other way.

343 The country has imploded. The Iraqis are suffocating. They want to travel, to open up to others. The regime makes concessions, but not enough.

Tariq Aziz
طارق عزيز
(April 28, 1936–
June 5, 2015)
Iraqi politician,
former Minister
of Foreign Affairs
under Saddam
Hussein.

344 On September 14, 2002, #TarikAziz appears on television, stating that Iraq has rejected the conditions of disarmament imposed by the Bush administration.

345 The day after September 11, 2001, the neocons started pointing the finger at Iraq. But there was nothing that linked al-Qaeda with Saddam Hussein.

346 For my father, and for all the Iraqis in exile, it's obvious. War is coming. The question isn't *whether* but *when*.

347 As time passes, the threat becomes more and more clear. Rhetoric becomes harsher. From this point on, war seems inevitable.

348 At home, my parents are worried. It's hard to imagine a world after Saddam. That still seemed impossible.

349 Even though my father was persecuted by Saddam Hussein, he was not in favor of this war. He knows too well what's at stake, strategically, and all the lies that are coming.

350 It might seem like a no-brainer for an Iraqi who hasn't lived under his dictatorship or even had a real taste of it. Still, I'm against military intervention.

351   When I'm on the phone with my family in Iraq, I think I can hear some hope in their voices: *I mean, what if the Americans really did come to liberate us?*

352   Many Iraqis felt they should benefit from globalization. The wars and twelve years under the embargo have swayed them.

353   That is, perhaps, the strategy at the heart of the embargo. Destroy Iraqi morale so that they are ready to be "liberated." A psychological prelude to war.

354   I'm still in journalism school in Paris when the first bombs rain down on Baghdad that terrible night on Thursday, March 20, 2003.

355   I can't watch the footage on TV. It reminds me of that winter evening in 1991. My father on his feet in front of the television, weeping for his brothers.

356   I don't want to see those "fireworks" in the skies over Baghdad. I hop on the subway. On line 7. I'm roaming aimlessly trying to forget the war.

357   I think about my family. About everyone I spent time with in Baghdad and Fallujah. What will be left of my country, of my childhood memories, when all of this is over?

358   The train stops at the Sully-Morland station. I'm sitting there, deep in thought, when a woman boards with a microphone in hand. She is lugging a wooden speaker behind her.

359   It's 11 p.m. She stands in front of me and says a few words before she starts to sing.

360   Her eyes meet mine. "This song is a tribute to the women and children of Iraq who are being bombarded as I speak." I can't believe it.

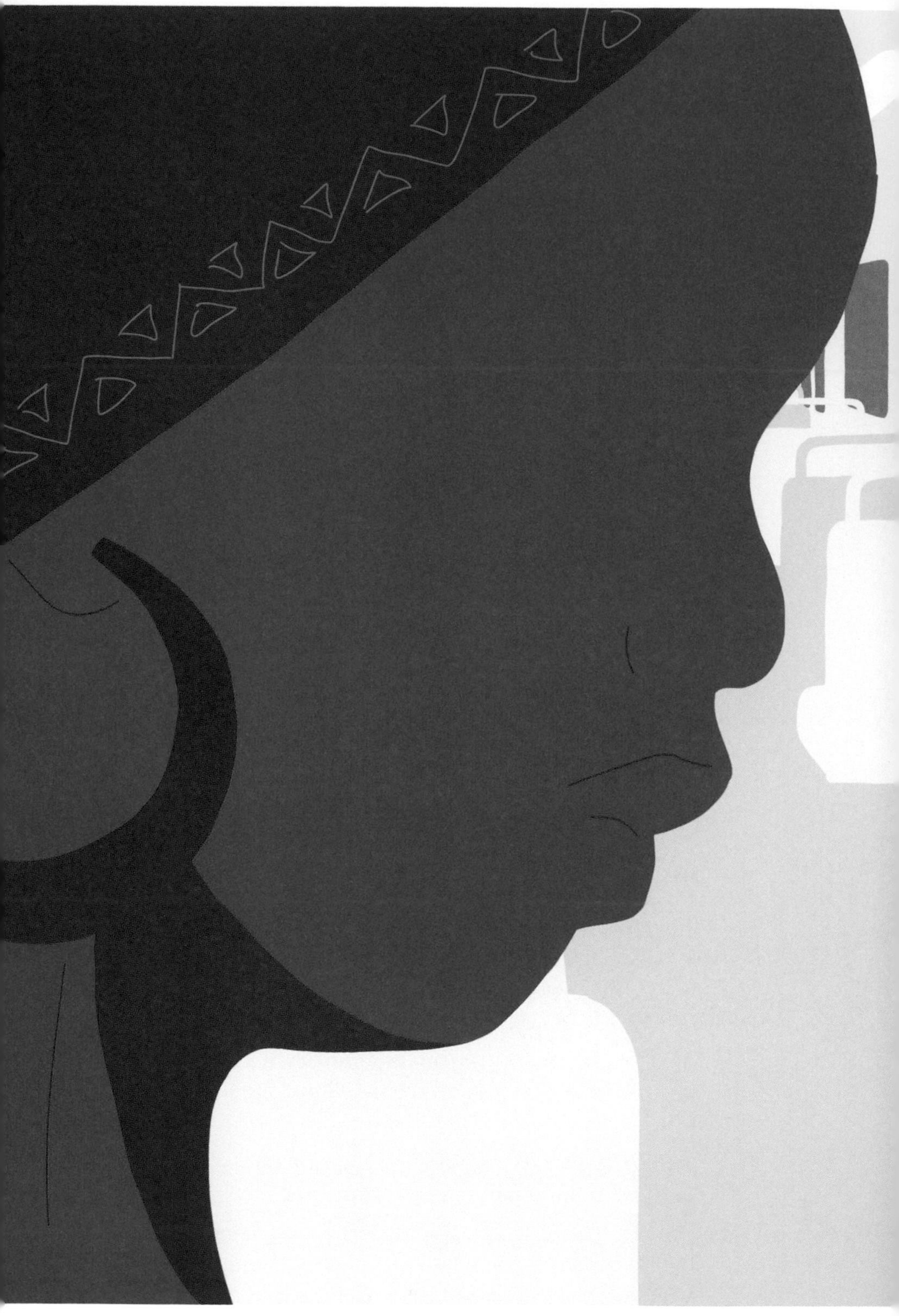

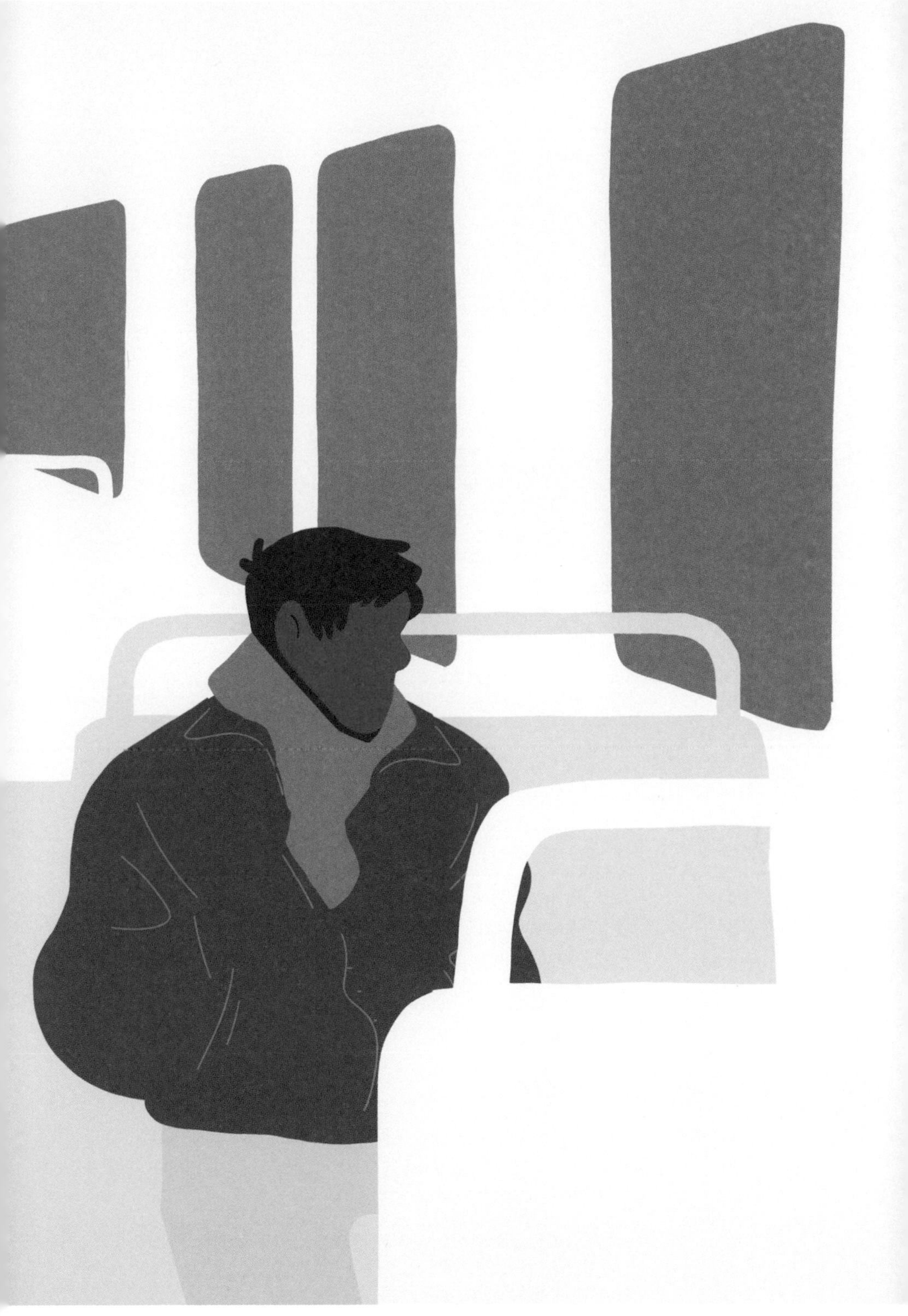

361　I ride the subway aimlessly to escape Iraq. And still it finds me. It's a miracle. The song speaks of freedom and of stars. It's 11 p.m., and Baghdad is burning.

362　The song ends. She sees that I'm moved. I thank her and tell her that I'm from Iraq. She smiles.

363　I give her everything I have in my wallet. Tears stream down her face. She gets out when the train reaches the Opéra station. I go home.

364　The days pass, and the invasion of Iraq progresses. The American tanks have to make their way north through southern Iraq. Umm Qasr is the port of entry.

365　It's the first savage act of resistance by the Iraqi army. The battle there lasts four days. Four days that feel like four years.

366　I'm visiting my parents in Nanterre one evening. The al-Jazeera network runs horrific footage from Basra. It's March 25, 2003.

367　The camera films the inside of a hospital that's been destroyed by American missiles. The charred bodies of dead children are scattered in the debris. Without a blur filter. On the ground.

368　The head on one of these bodies is partially ripped off. A little body strewn in the rubble like an abandoned doll.

369　My mother weeps. My father remains silent. Absolutely furious, I get up and go to the bathroom. I punch a hole in the door with my fist.

370　I am overcome with anger, by the powerlessness I feel and the injustice of it all. There's no greater suffering than that caused by injustice.

371 I see myself crying in the mirror. Guilt is the essence of anger. That child could have been a cousin, a sister. Or me. I'm overwhelmed.

372 The only way to stop the useless suffering is to go there. To start my career sooner than I had planned. I want to go to Baghdad.

373 At school they told me to get an internship. I ask to see the program director. I'll do my internship in Baghdad, or not at all.

374 I board the Iraqi Airways plane. In 1989, I was lucky enough to get a tour of the cockpit. The pilot was my cousin's husband.

375 This time, I'm alone. Yesterday I called on as many editorial teams as I could. They looked me up and down. They smiled at me.

376 From the plane's window, Baghdad seems frozen in time. Just like my memories of this moment. I don't know what state I'll find it (or myself) in.

377 The plane descends, circling down like a falling leaf before landing. That's to avoid a possible missile attack. The pilot speaks with a South African accent.

378 Heading to the taxi stand, I recognize the plastic stalactite lighting in the ceiling of the departures terminal. I flash back to the one hundred waving hands that greeted me here in 1989. Hello solitude.

379 Around me, I see American soldiers for the first time. Their combat helicopters were on the tarmac. *Apocalypse Now* in Baghdad.

380 It feels strange to no longer feel at home here. The occupation is marked by a very visible American military presence.

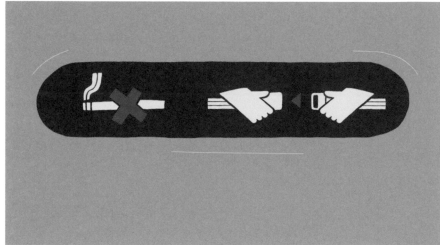

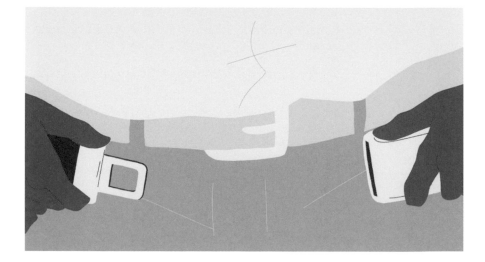

Abbas ibn Firnas
عباس بن فرناس
(810–887)
Inventor, doctor,
and poet of Berber
origin. Born in
Izn-Rand Onda
al-Andalus (today
known as Ronda, in
Spain), he lived in
the Emirate of Cór-
doba and is known
for trying to fly.

The World's Most
Dangerous Road
Twelve-kilometer
highway linking the
Baghdad Inter-
national Airport
with the "Green
Zone," the heavily
fortified area in the
center of Baghdad.
Also called "Route
Irish" by American
soldiers because of
the daily bombings
along the route.

381 I pick up a chartered taxi at the airport. He drops me at the foot of the #AbbasIbnFirnas statue of the inventor and the very first pilot in history.

382 From there, I take a traditional taxi to Mansour. We head onto Baghdad Airport Road, dubbed by the Americans #TheWorldsMostDangerousRoad.

383 My drive to Mansour is a story in itself. There are traces of war everywhere. The renowned restaurant al-Sa'a has been destroyed. I reach my aunt's house.

384 I plan to stay for a while in the house in Mansour. My aunt Soumaya opens the door. My uncle-in-law Aziz and my cousins Ziaya and Mahmud are there.

385 The garden hasn't changed. Nor the gardener, Hussein. He lives in the Sadr City district. We often talk about Iraq. I like him very much.

386 Hussein is, above all, a friend. He will also be a trustworthy source for me and be my guide in Sadr City. A "fixer," in journalistic lingo.

387 At dinner my cousins admit that they really don't understand. Why did I come to Iraq when they, them-selves, aren't sure whether they should stay or leave?

388 Our conversation is interrupted by the noise of American helicopters flying over the house, always in pairs. . . .

389 The noise in Baghdad is what strikes me the most. You can get a feeling for the occupation of a country in different ways. For me, it's in the noise of helicopters.

390 Just about every thirty minutes, the Chinooks hover overhead. They're taunting us. They remind us of the occupation.

391 My uncle has a small residence on the property. Mahmud's group of sullen friends are gathered in his little shack. They're drinking.

392 And playing cards. They're eating *pacha,* or sheep's stomach. A dish reserved for men, real men. They play rummy until morning.

393 The hut serves as a headquarters for some pretty shady guys. There's an enormous man who's 6'4" and at least 286 pounds. He's said to have killed a woman for her gold.

Paul Bremer (September 30, 1941–) American diplomat who was appointed the civil administrator in Iraq in May 2003. He was nicknamed the "Governor of Baghdad."

394 The Bush administration appoints #PaulBremer to govern Iraq. Bremer wears the suit of a politician and the combat boots of a soldier.

395 People are already calling him "Saddam Bremer." He gives a thumbs-up or a thumbs-down whenever he feels like it. His first decision? Dissolve the Ba'ath Party.

396 "Order no. 2" sends Iraq into chaos. Bremer discharges the entire Iraqi military, putting a million people out on the street.

Green Zone المنطقة الخضراء Heavily fortified enclave in the Iraqi city of Baghdad, established in April of 2003 as a result of the persistent fighting and bombings. Most Iraqi and foreign diplomats live in the Green Zone, which is also referred to as the international zone.

397 A complete and arbitrary purge. Outside the #GreenZone, which is under the control of the American military, protesters demand work. Peacefully.

398 In May 2003, American soldiers were still walking about freely in the streets, lining up at restaurants and talking to people.

399 But the civility is short-lived. In Fallujah a couple days ago, the Americans fired on a crowd of unarmed protesters.

400 It's the start of an insurrection. The peaceful protesters will take up arms. Iraq is going to move from liberation to occupation.

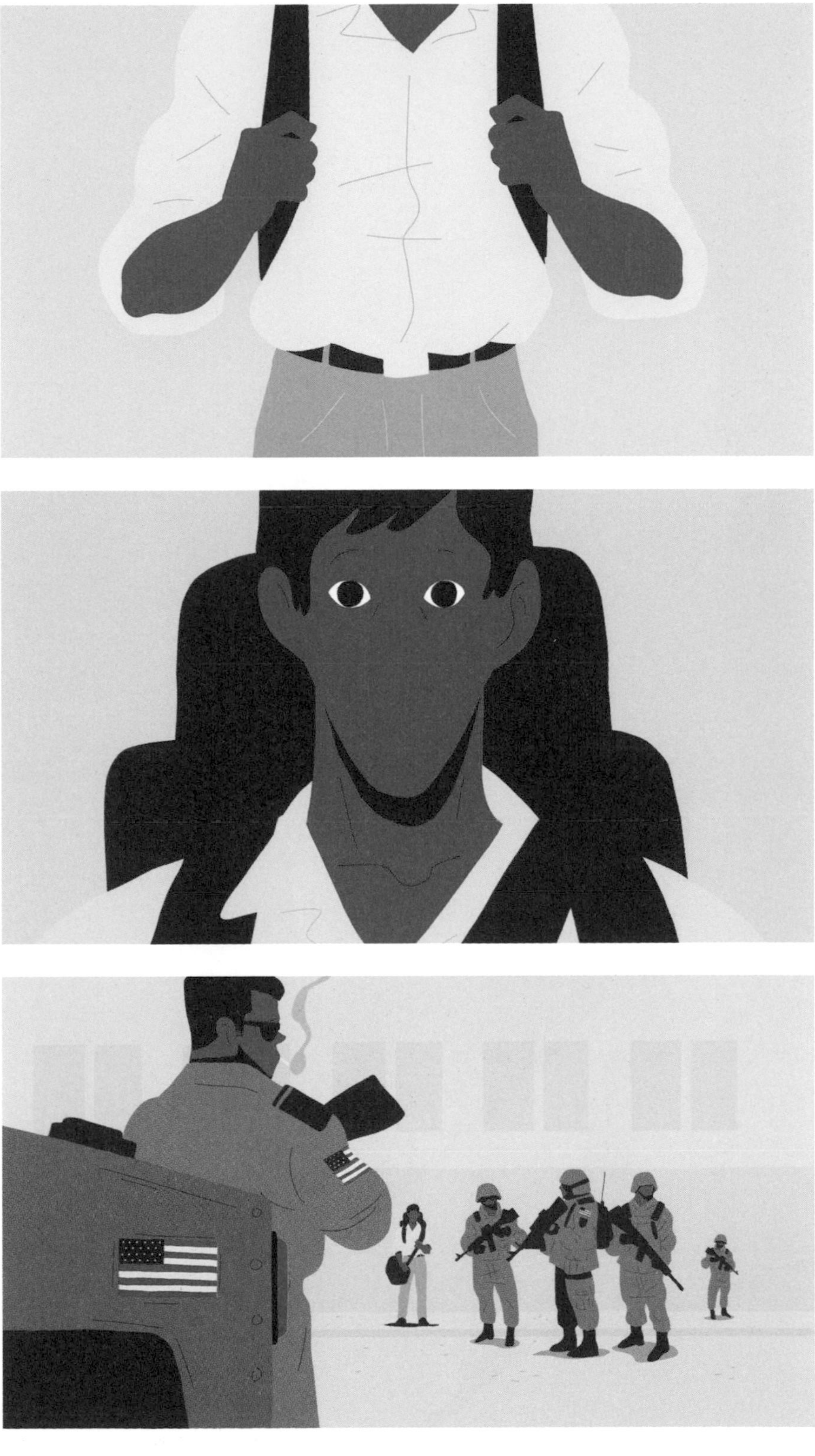

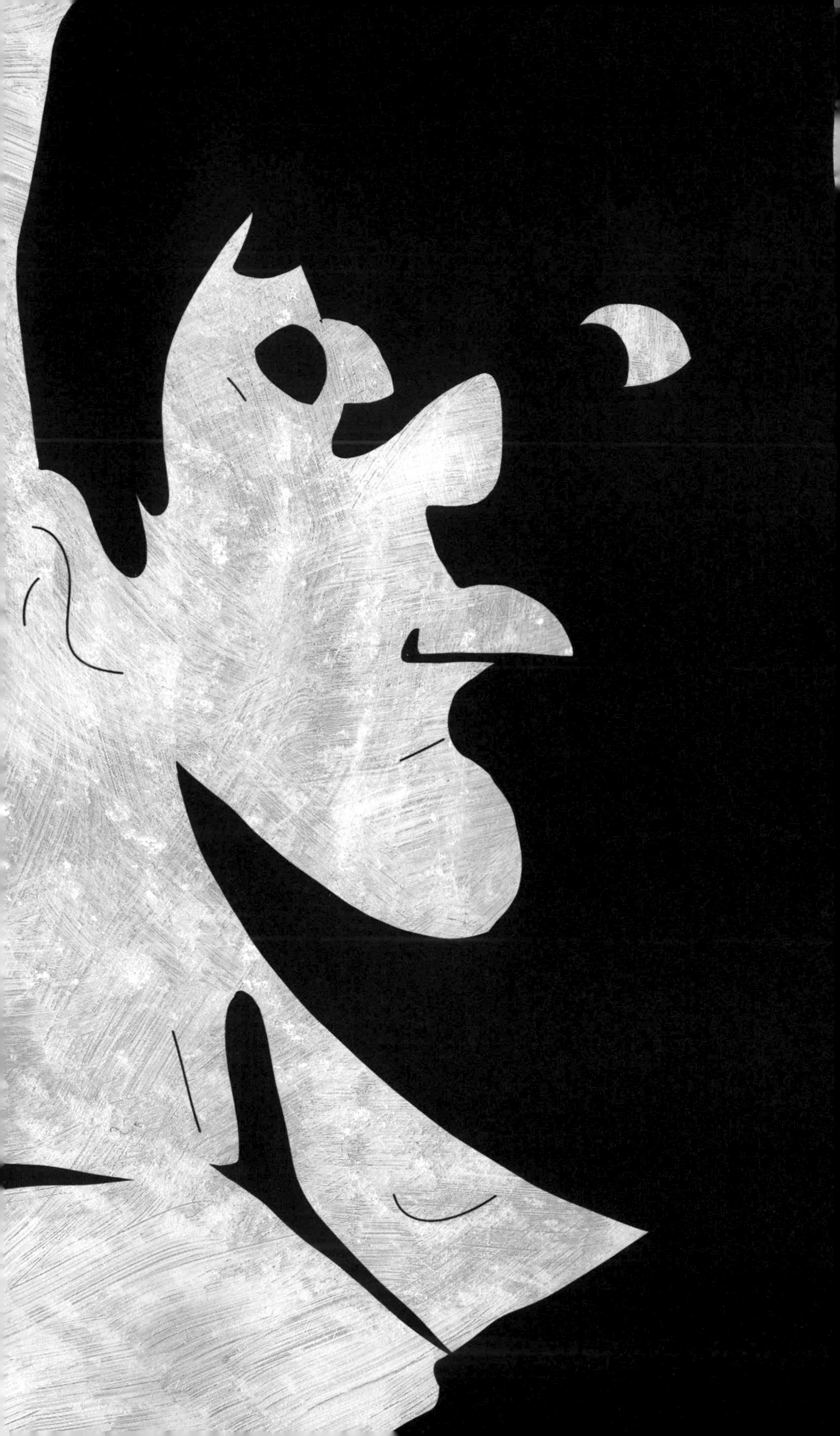

2003 This is how I write my first news stories. Embedded with family going about their daily routines.

401 I wrote about the noise of war. The helicopters. In the summer of 2003, you could add to that the sound of bomb blasts, gunshots, and sirens.

402 These are the sounds of Baghdad. Sometimes I'd hear covert attacks on the corner of my street in Mansour. The rhythmic sound of gun shots responding to gun shots.

403 That evening, armed men swarmed into my street to attack the neighborhood's main checkpoint—an operation that lasted for a full fifteen minutes.

404 Fifteen minutes of hell. We turned off the lights in our front room. The sound of gunfire resonates deeply within us. My cousin sobs.

405 It's as if the fighting is happening inside our house. With each flash, I see fear in the faces around me.

406 We're now facing a different kind of battle—that of fighting off the panic. Keeping our composure. I hope no armed men come in here.

407 Then there's silence. We turn the lights back on. Then the television. And still this silence. Five of us in a room not speaking to one another.

408 Maybe there's no need to speak to come to terms with these kinds of events. Luckily, the house wasn't hit by gunfire.

409 Not a single day passes without hearing explosions. That evening, there's a massive explosion. I hug the wall to keep from falling.

410 An explosion just a couple doors from here. The Jordanian embassy was targeted by a truck bomb. Tomorrow I'll go take a photo.

411 I head over to see my aunt Khamael in the Amiriya district in western Baghdad. I plan to stay a week. I meet up with my cousin Mazen.

412 Amiriya is still where you find the most residents from Fallujah and Ramadi. The neighborhood hasn't changed.

413 The streets are a lot dirtier. Garbage piles up on every street corner, and no one seems to care. Mazen is hungry.

414 The business strip is filled with falafel huts. You can also find sweetened turnips in broth there. They warm you up in the winter.

415 During the day, life goes on somewhat normally, without a lot of stress. Except for the helicopters overhead that constantly remind us of where we are.

416 At night, it's another story. A lot of insurrection operations are centered on Amiyira. The inescapable noise of war.

417 That evening, as Mazen and I are heading home from the market, we see a run-down BMW with four guys inside.

418 The BMW passes us. At the end of the street there's a police station. The car stops at the corner. Gunfire. Squealing of tires.

419 These four men just attacked the police station with Kalashnikovs before roaring off. We pick up the pace to get home.

420 These kinds of missions happen every day. One of the kids I played soccer with in 1989 was supposedly in that group.

421 Mazen is busy with medical school. He tells me the morgue is overcrowded now because more and more people are getting killed.

422 Interns practice medicine as early as their first year. They are in operating rooms and in morgues. They're in the war. Exhausted.

423 Mazen is sometimes at the hospital for 24 hours straight. Where they stitched me up in 1995. Only 100,000 dinars for anesthesia.

424 Today he is the one doing the stitching. He describes unbearable scenes. "You get used to it quickly. We even eat snacks in the morgue."

425 I don't yet feel ready to go with him to the hospital. I don't want to see the blood or hear the screams. One day soon, I'm sure.

426 I go with Mazen's brother, Firas, to the Jamila district, an industrial area in eastern Baghdad. It's the port of entry to Sadr City.

427 He's in the import-export business. It's a dream of Iraqis who don't have a degree to work in international trade for a percentage of the profits.

428 But to do that you need *wasta*—connections. According to Firas, the holy grail of connections is the government. Working with them pays well.

429 Sugar. Flour. Chicken. Tires. Whatever it is you need. If you have access to *wasta* in the government, you'll find the holy grail.

430 This is how I write my first news stories. Embedded with family going about their daily routines. Rubbing shoulders with Iraqis. Getting to know them.

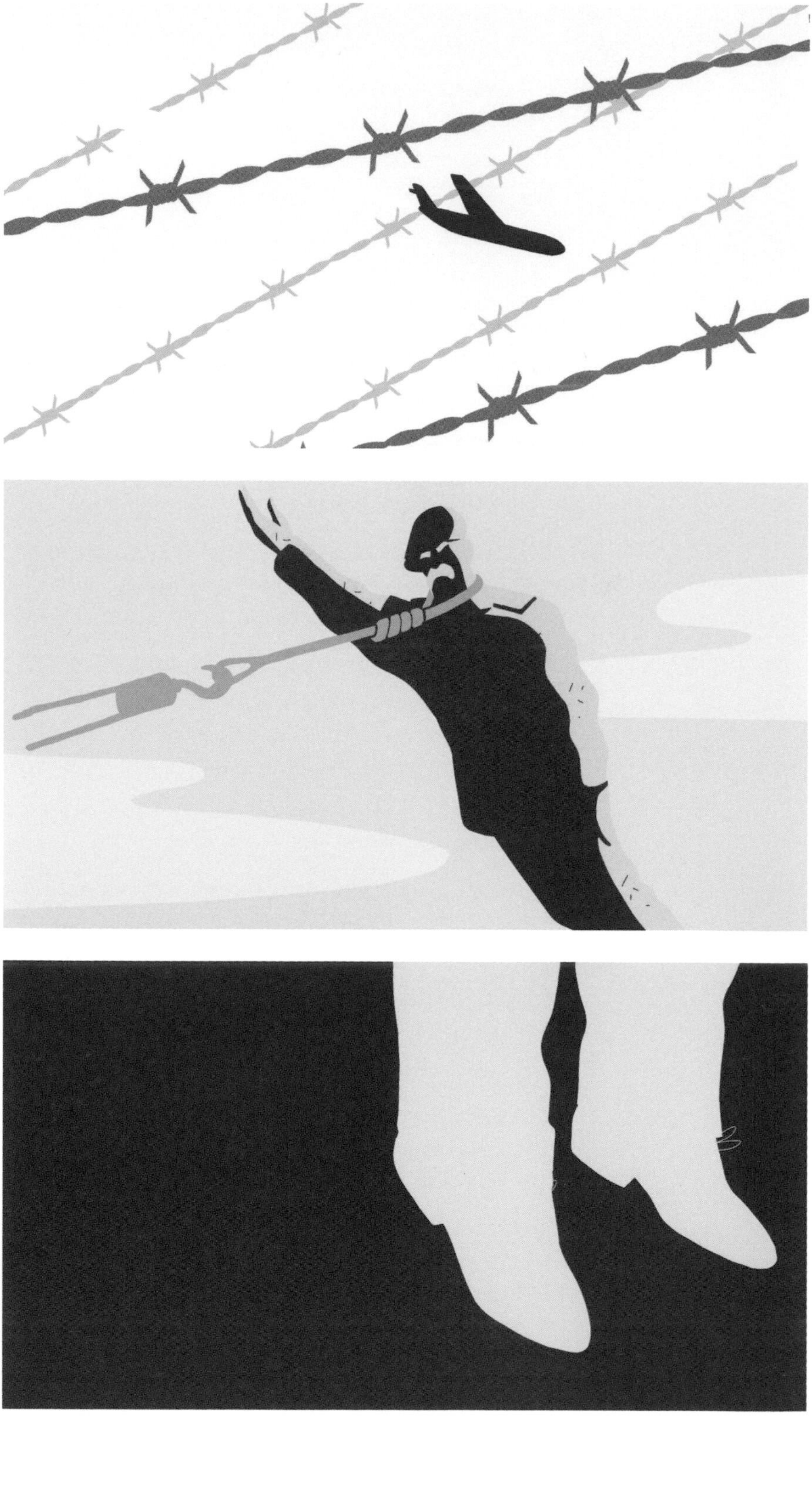

431 The news just dropped. Saddam Hussein has been captured near Tikrit, on the outskirts of al-Awja, where he was born. They found him "in a hole."

432 In a news conference, Paul Bremer confirms this: "We got him." Applause. Cheers. Whistles. Insults. It's December 2003.

433 In recent months, a bunch of rumors were circulating about Saddam. Some saw him walking around Tikrit. Others in Adhamiya, in the mosque.

434 The legendary bravado of Saddam Hussein was so deeply entrenched in the minds of Iraqis that it was hard to imagine him hiding in a hole in the ground.

435 For many, this image put an end to the myth. Whether you're a victim, an enemy, or in the inner circle, Saddam's downfall is a strange event.

436 My father was a victim of the *rais*. We had no connection to him and weren't part of the elite. And yet I can't help but feel sad.

437 What will become of Iraq after thirty-five years of dictatorship? Why do I have this ominous feeling that his end is the beginning of a nightmare?

Stockholm Syndrome Psychological phenomenon observed in hostages who have been with their captors for a long period of time and who have developed a sort of empathy with them, for reasons having to do with complex mechanisms of identification and survival.

438 Saddam is inseparable from the Iraq I knew. Everything that happened was because of him. It was as if his mood set the tone for the day.

439 A terrifying figure, to be sure. He was a part of our lives. We were taken hostage, even when abroad. Maybe it was #StockholmSyndrome.

440 In 1989, you weren't allowed to say his name. Fifteen years later, I am going to write it, voice it, express it, discuss it. It's the turning of a page.

441 I'm back in Mansour at my aunt's house, my home base. It's a house full of memories. But today, it's empty.

442 My aunt and uncle have gone to live in Jordan. It's now just my two cousins, Mahmud and Ziad. And Hussein, the gardener from Sadr City, is here, too.

443 It's New Year's Eve. The year 2003 was a turning point. Tonight the skies over large cities are bursting with light, and yet ours remains black.

444 On televisions throughout the world people are watching the countdown. We're watching a story about a car bomb that targeted an American convoy. An eight-year-old Iraqi child is dead.

445 American soldiers no longer walk in the streets. They no longer line up at restaurants. They're holed up at their posts.

446 They drive around in their convoys with absolute contempt for everything in their path. They ram into cars, saying "fuck" and "haji."

447 By 2004, there is no more interaction on the street between American soldiers and Iraqis. Every resident is suspected of being an insurgent.

448 One of Mazen's friends suffered this fate. He was crossing the street holding a cell phone to his ear when an American convoy passed by. One shot. Right to his head.

449 A cell phone can be a potential detonator for an IED. No warning shots were fired. The soldier took aim. The *haji* was taken down.

450 That was the tipping point. From then on, American convoys put up a sign: "Keep Back 100 Meters." And whatever you do, don't make a phone call.

451 February 2004. After a couple of months, I go back to Paris to resume my coursework. To come back down. And meet with editors.

452 The long months I spent in Baghdad in isolation forced me to internalize. It's crazy how quickly you adapt to being at war.

453 Everyone externalizes their experiences in one way or another when they're back home. Anxiety attacks, crying, depression for some. As for me, I don't know yet.

454 I find a table in a café in the Beaubourg neighborhood of Paris. It's too crowded here. I'm not used to this. My head is spinning. Coffee, check, and bolt.

455 In Baghdad, I wrote my first articles for *Le Soir,* the well-known Belgian newspaper, and *Le Point.* My first byline is a point of pride.

456 The first article I wrote during my "internship" was read by many. People congratulated me. They framed my article from *Le Soir.* It was my trophy.

457 Now I'm writing for *Ouest-France,* one of the five major dailies in France. I will become their Baghdad correspondent. It's a huge opportunity.

458 I realize there's a discrepancy between the images we see on TV and the reality on the ground. Sure, Iraq is at war. But life goes on, too.

459 Iraq isn't just about counting up the dead. Nor is it just a morgue. You have to tell the story of all the death here, yes. But above all, you have to tell the story of life.

460 The country code +964 turns up on my cell phone. It's my uncle Riyad from Fallujah. He has news about the family. Some things have changed.

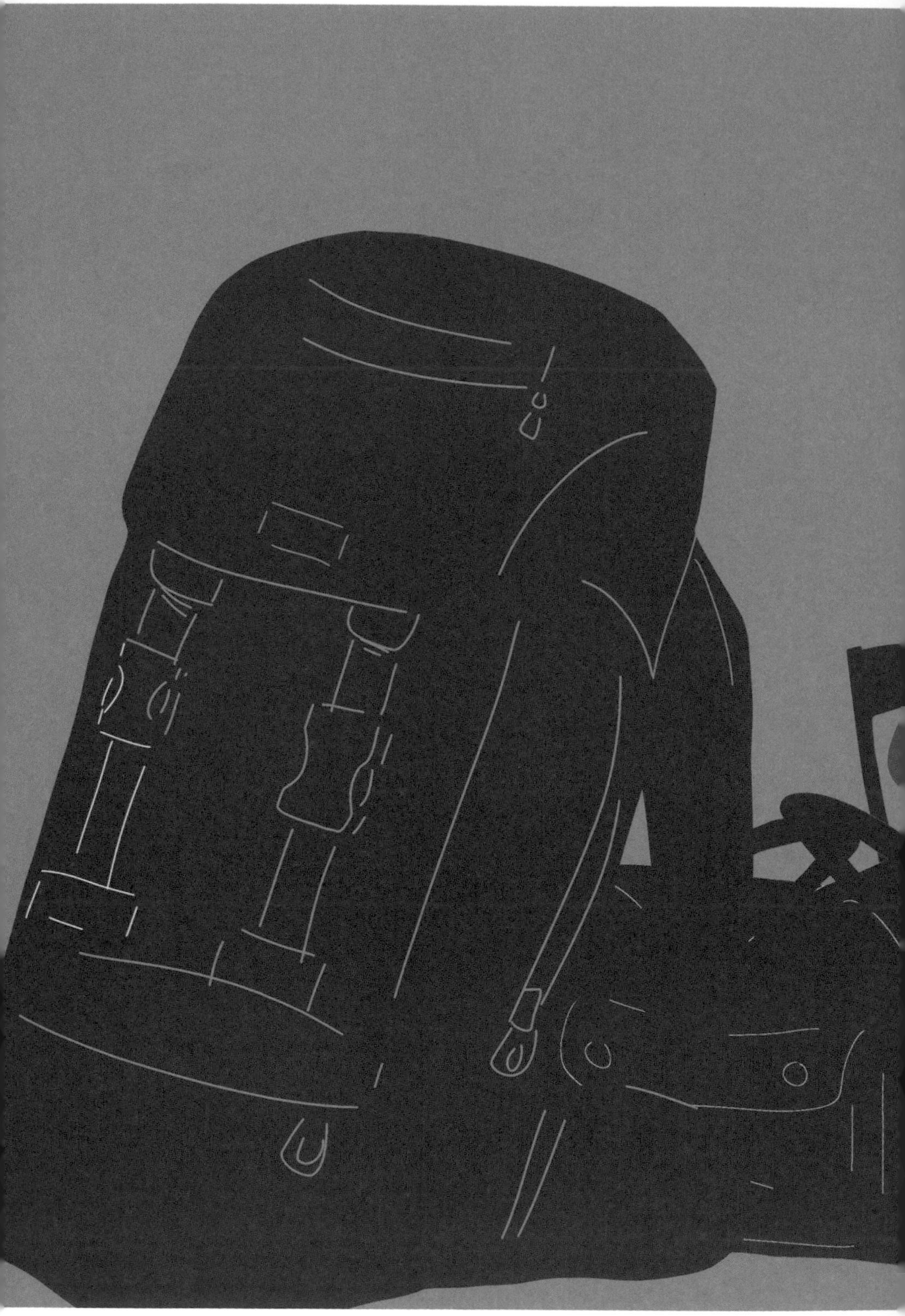

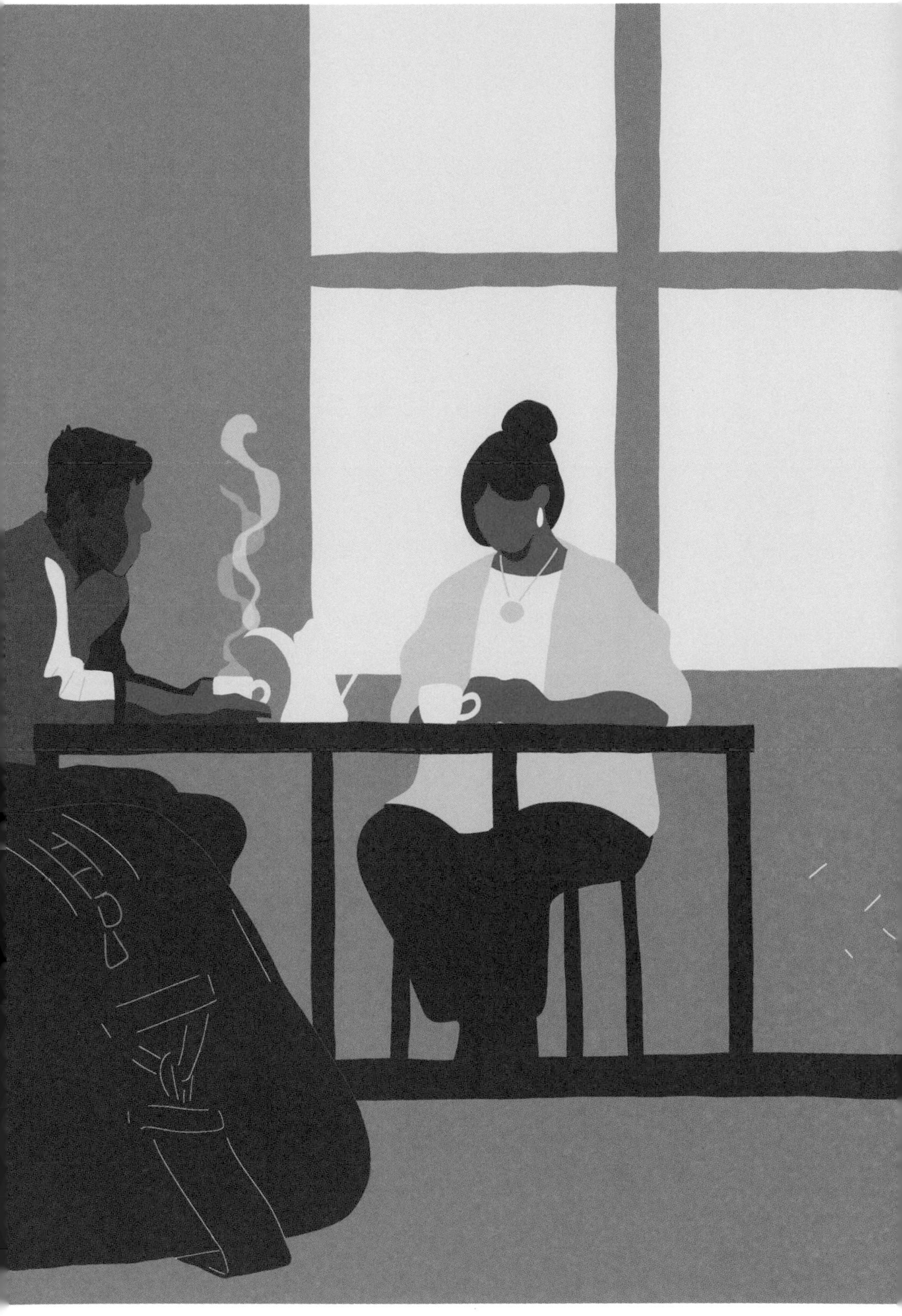

461 Paris → Amman. Amman → Baghdad. The road of death to Amiriya. Springtime in Iraq is flush with bombs. In Fallujah, it's winter.

462 The first thing that strikes me is Fallujah's new moniker: *madinat al-masajid* the city of mosques. They're everywhere. At least 300 of them.

463 I see Uncle Riyad. He has aged. His wrinkles are accentuated by his sad green eyes. Ahmed has been arrested.

464 My cousin Ahmed, the one who looks like Mike Tyson, transported crates of vegetables to the Fallujah market during the embargo.

Mujahidin
مُجَاهِدِين
Islamic militants who joined the insurgency after the 2003 invasion of Iraq to engage in *jihad,* or the fight against the unfaithful.

465 The latest crates he was transporting were full of weapons. In April 2004, Ahmed was a member of the #*Mujahidin*. Working in logistics.

466 He was arrested by American soldiers when he tried to pass through a checkpoint with a crate full of weapons. He was done for.

467 Ahmed was imprisoned at #AbuGhraib before being transferred to #CampBucca in southern Iraq. Visitors weren't allowed.

Abu Ghraib
سجن أبو غريب
Main prison in Baghdad, made infamous by the torture American soldiers and CIA agents inflicted on Iraqi prisoners.

468 I had just missed Ahmed. He left behind his mother—my aunt Khawla—and her other son. Aunt Khawla is heartbroken.

469 What could I do? There was no way for me to get into the prison at Camp Bucca, in spite of my French nationality. Yet another tragedy in Iraq.

Camp Bucca
سجن بوكا
American military prison situated in southern Iraq, which closed in 2009.

470 Uncle Riyad told me that my uncles were also fighting the fight. Each one in a different group. Ordinary citizens by day, masked militants by night.

471 With "emperor" Paul Bremer now gone, Ayad Allawi steps in. He was an opposition leader before cycling through the Ba'ath Party, the CIA, and MI6. The new face of Iraq.

472 It's the Iraq of car bombs, before there were militia groups. The insurrection intensifies. Seventy-five attacks per day throughout the country.

473 Explosions and gunshots every twenty minutes. When a car bomb exploded five kilometers from where I was standing, I felt the earth shake.

474 I do my work for *Ouest-France* during the summer of 2004. Portrayals of everyday life, starting with my cousin Mazen at the Yarmouk hospital.

475 Profession: MD in Baghdad. "Seeing bodies blown to pieces and skulls with gaping holes is really hard." Some doctors can't hack it. Mazen sticks it out.

476 The interns are searched at the hospital entrance. Today, the hospital courtyard is surprisingly calm.

477 Blood marks on the walls are signs of the devastating brutality seen here on some days. Mazen works with fifteen interns, men and women.

478 Just like at university, the hospital is a place where boys flirt discreetly with girls. Affairs of love and death.

479 Mazen tells me about the day a car exploded at the police station in al-Qadisiyyah, near the hospital. The first wave of the wounded. The blood.

480 Many of the injured were treated right on the ground because the operating room had only twenty beds. Mazen kept his emotions in check.

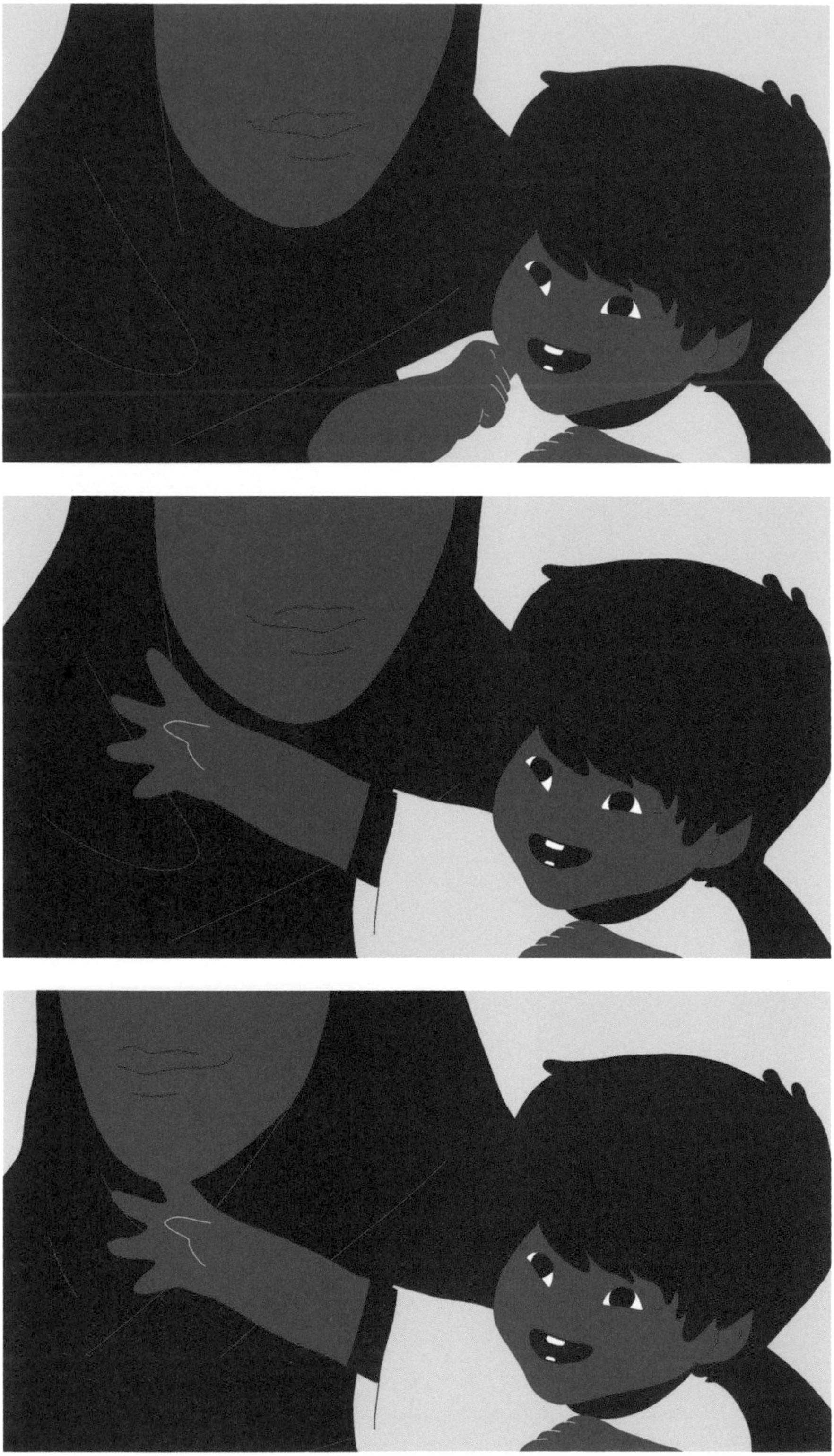

481 I spend the month of Ramadan in Baghdad in 2004, in Amiriya. It's the middle of October. The heat is gone.

Wahhabism
وهابية
A reform movement within Sunni Islam originating in the 18th century in Nadjid, the central part of what is known today as Saudi Arabia. Founded by Muhammad ibn Abd al-Wahhab (1703–1792), Wahhabism is a form of fundamentalism that calls for a return to the original sources of Islam (the Koran and the Hadith) and insists on the absolute oneness of God.

482 It's my first experience fasting in a Muslim-majority country. Aunt Khamael is here. We call her the *#wahhabite* because she's very pious.

483 There are my cousins Mazen, Firas, Hasna, and Nour. And the neighbor's cat. The house is full of prayers and religious fervor.

484 At dawn, we're awakened by beating drums. *Boom Badaboom*. "Better to pray than sleep! Wake up!"

485 The drummers march from district to district. The scene is surreal. Magical. Getting out of bed is rough. Hasna is always the last.

486 I have a strong sensation of being shaken awake. Reminds me of a car bomb. My aunt says it was an angel that woke me.

487 Aunt Khamael reads the Koran. On the table there are dates, *labneh*—a kind of fermented cheese—water, and eggs. I eat with my eyes closed.

488 And I sleep with my eyes open. What a strange month of devoutness in a country that is being ravaged by a war with no name, front, or religion.

489 The next day we go to the Omar Mosque in Amiriya. The government has accused the imam of preaching against the Americans. He is sobbing.

490 On the way out, the worshippers go to him to offer comfort. A "Sunni" imam. And a "Shiite" government. A war of denominations is on the horizon.

491   The Battle of Fallujah in November 2004 is one of the fiercest urban battles the world has seen. It is often likened to the Battle of Hue during the Vietnam War.

492   I couldn't get into the city during the battle. As soon as it ends, I go straight to Uncle Saad's. He lives in the Askari district on the front line.

493   His house is destroyed, just like 80% of the city. Fallujah looks like the moon. Everything is gray. Dusty. People's faces, too.

494   We are at the Martyrs' Cemetery, formerly a soccer field. I played there in 1992. Today, instead of netted goals there are tombstones.

495   Two of my cousins are buried there. They fought against the Americans. They were 16 and 17. Buried right where they had once played. We recite the *fatiha*—the first *surah*, or chapter, of the Koran.

496   There are 3,000 tombs there, including one grouping that gets more visitors than the others. Twenty-nine slabs. An entire family was obliterated by a missile.

497   The Martyrs' Cemetery. A depressing symbol. My uncles join us. I know they fought, too. We don't speak—not yet.

498   Someone says the sky has changed color, that white phosphorus is falling on civilians, that strange weapons are being used.

499   I don't know what they're talking about at this point. Maybe it's too soon to talk about it. I make a note: "White phosphorus." "Orange sky."

500   I want to know what happened in Fallujah in November 2004. I'll reopen that file eventually. But now is the time for mourning.

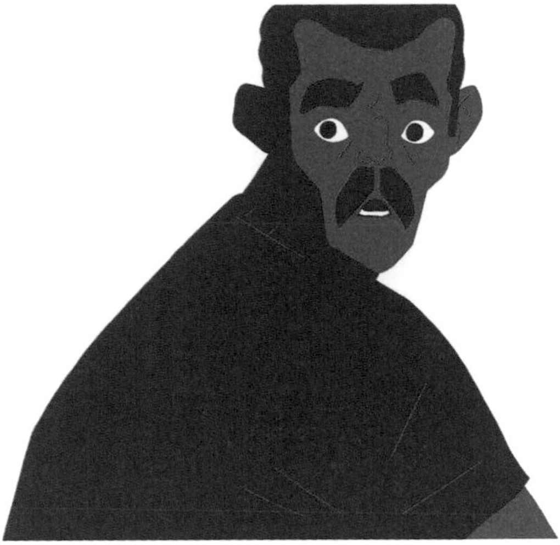

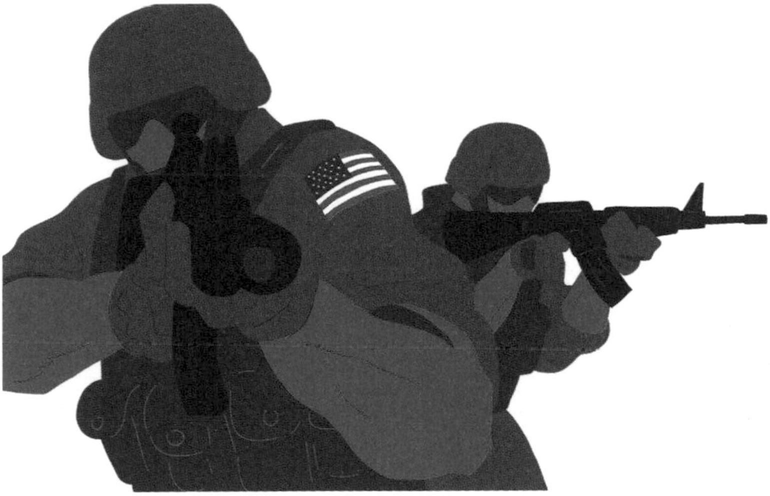

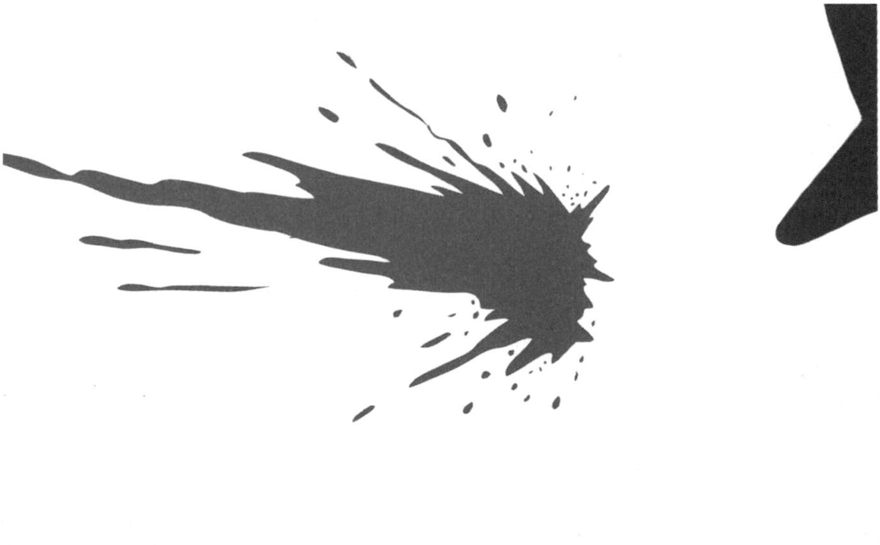

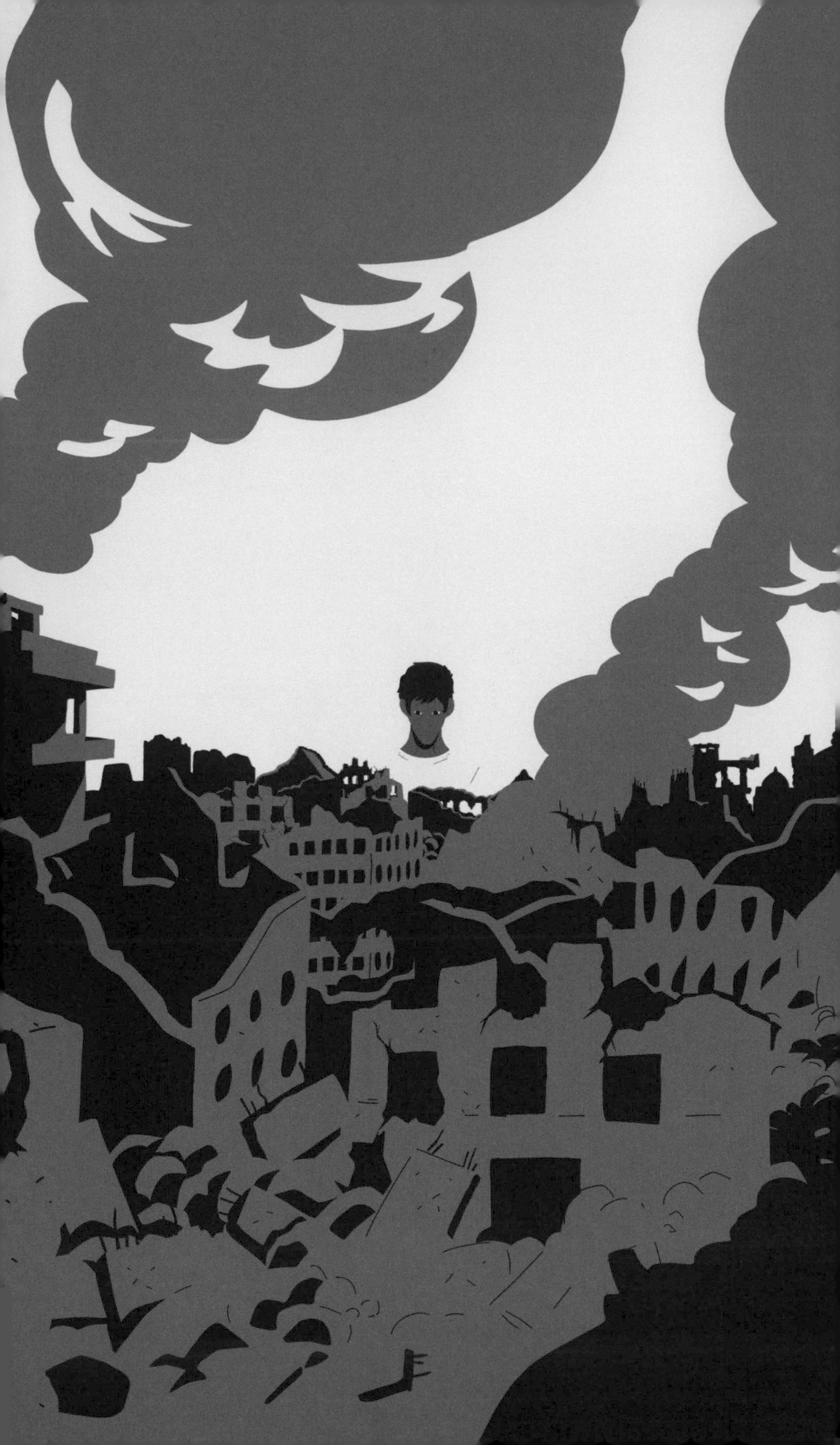

The IED: inside the house, the foundation shakes. Out on the street, a blast of hot air in your face.

501 The city of Fallujah is demolished. Few houses are left standing. Some had to bury their loved ones in the garden. They live, survive, in a cemetery.

502 The family home of *Bibi* Samia was hit by a shell. There's a hole in the roof. A few points of impact. But the house withstood the shock.

503 *Bibi* Samia is as talkative as ever. My uncles stand up straight and even manage to joke a little. I sit down next to Uncle Imad, the smiling poet.

Salafism
السلفية
A branch of Sunni Islam advocating for a return to the ways of life of "the pious predecessors," or the Muslims who lived at the time of the Prophet Mohamed and his disciples.

504 He shares what he saw of the Battle of Fallujah. Imad is an adherent of #Salafism. Each of my uncles belongs to a different group.

505 One of them is part of a militant Sufi organization, another is a nationalist. Each knows what the other is doing. But no one talks about it, out of respect.

506 One evening, Imad is in position on a roof. He and some others are in a violent gunfight with the marines that will last several hours.

507 A magical moment: Imad says, with absolute certainty, that a celestial army of white pigeons was sent to them to counter the shots from the Americans.

508 His eyes shine. He is silent and pensive. Imad describes these white pigeons—"angels"—hurling themselves at the bullets to protect them.

509 I chalked that up to his emotions, a fervor bordering on religious mania. It made me sad. And then I smiled at the poet.

510 I'll always have that image of my uncle lying prostrate on a roof and shooting off rounds, saved by his "angels" from heaven. He is still alive, after all.

511 Then, one day, I read *The Forever War* by Dexter Filkins, a journalist embedded with the American military in November 2004 during the Battle of Fallujah.

512 Page 204 and following: "The geese came in from the north, flying in a slightly broken V, as the fighting of southern Fallujah unfolded below. . . ."

513 "As the birds approached, they appeared unable to alter their course. They kept flying until they were directly over the fighting."

514 "There was machine-gun fire, then an explosion. . . . The V dissolved into a tangle of confused circles, the birds veering past each other in the sky . . ."

515 ". . . seemingly trapped above the apocalypse below. . . . I watched the fighting a few blocks away, directly below the geese."

516 "A building exploded, sending up a tunnel of flame. . . . [T]he geese began to . . . re-form into their broken V. Then they turned to the southwest and continued on their way."

517 I closed the book. Then the image of my uncle Imad telling me with shining eyes about the arrival of the flying angels came to mind. They must have been geese.

518 My uncle Imad wasn't crazy. What he had told me was the truth. His truth. Dexter Filkins had his truth, too. Angels from the heavens, or migratory birds?

519 After all, it was really just a question of perception. One mystical, the other one rational. I couldn't believe it, and my heart ached.

520 Summed up in this vision of the geese was the gulf between the Iraqis and the Americans in Fallujah. Finding refuge in poetry was one way to survive.

521 I leave Fallujah in a state of deep sorrow. The city I had known in 1989 is no more. It's now a pile of grayish dust.

522 January 2005. In the Amiriya district of Baghdad, at least one car bomb explodes every day. I can start to distinguish the types of explosions.

523 The car bomb: You can feel the explosion deep inside even before hearing it. The shell: A clear and powerful sound. It shakes the windows.

524 The IED: Inside the house, the foundation shakes. Out on the street, a blast of hot air in your face. Grains of sand in your mouth.

525 Before going out on the street, most residents of Baghdad listen to the sounds of the city. It's the war-time way of life.

526 Flashes and smoke in the sky determine the exact route you'll take as you move around the capital. Even children recognize the sound of bombs.

527 Gunshots. The difference between an AK-47 and an M16? Easy. The former sounds like stuttering bursts: *Tatata-tatata-tata*. The latter is heavier and continuous: *TATATATATATA*.

528 Children don't play much soccer in the streets anymore. Now they play war. The most popular toys these days are the plastic AK-47 and the plastic grenade. No more soccer balls.

529 When a pair of helicopters flies overhead with that loud chopping sound, the children keep on playing without batting an eye. It's routine.

530 What will become of this war generation, born in Iraq during the embargo? And what of those who were born in 2003? How do we get through this horrific turmoil unscathed?

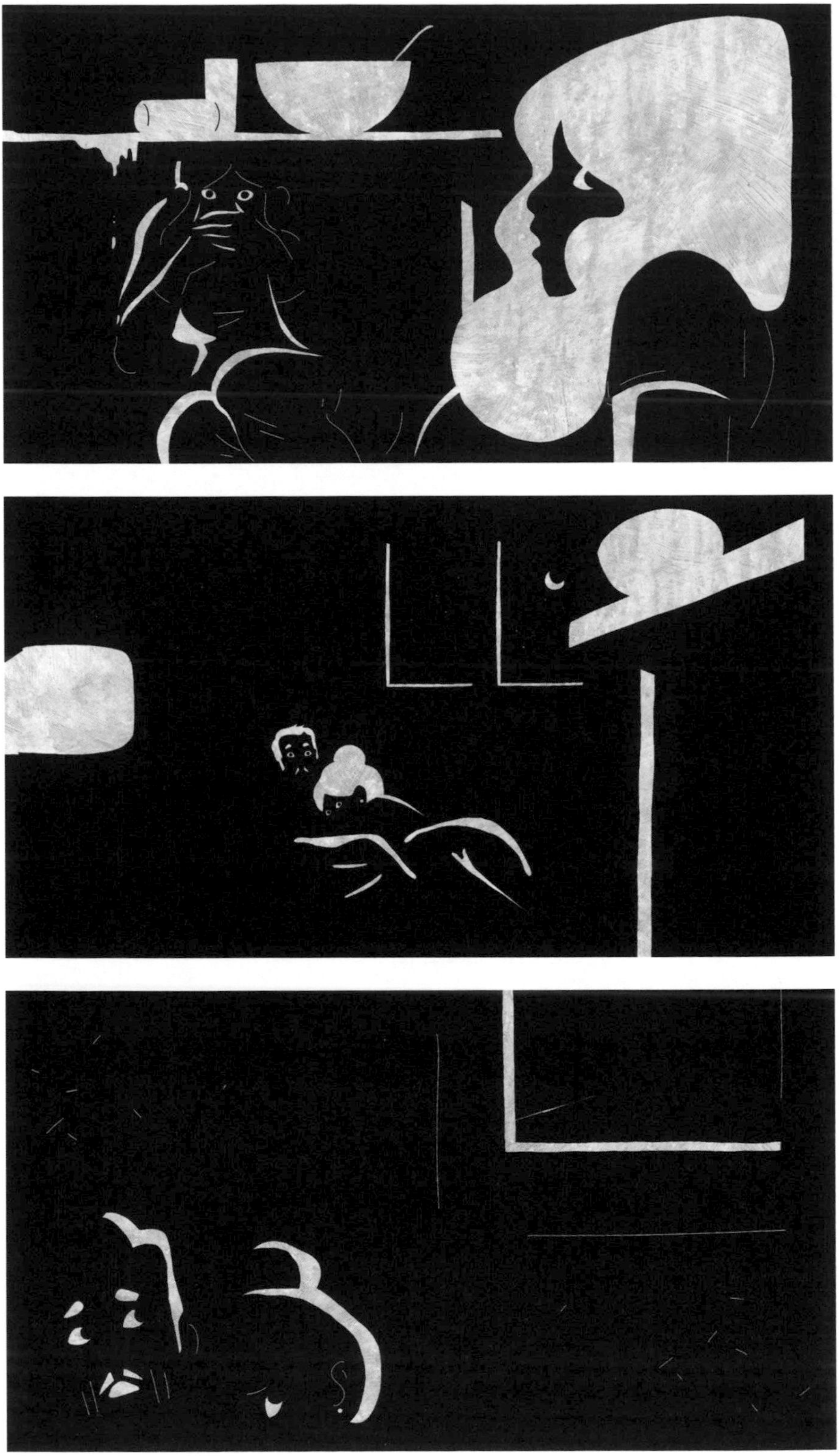

531 Winters in Baghdad are bitter. Iraqi homes tend to be large and airy, designed for the summer months. To keep warm, they use gasoline heaters.

532 These heaters also warm up the tea kettle, when placed on top. You sit in front of the glowing grill to stay warm.

533 My aunt's house is immense. It's impossible to keep out the cold with this little hand warmer. I live, eat, and sleep in the same room.

534 There's no one here anymore. My aunt and uncle have left. My cousin Mohamed, too. Before he left, he gave me his AK-47. . . .

535 Now, in 2005, a curfew is in place. No one is allowed out after 9 p.m. Mohamed told me to sleep with the submachine gun at my side.

536 "If someone shows up here after curfew, it's because something's not right. Here's how you load it," he had told me. I hoped I'd never have to use it.

537 The Kalashnikov sleeps next to me. I sleep facing the window, which looks out over the front entrance of the house. Everything is dark at night. The street, too.

538 Sometimes I ask myself what I'm doing here, alone, with a submachine gun, a laptop, and a hand warmer.

539 To keep warm, there's a special dish that Iraqis eat in winter: date syrup mixed with sesame oil.

540 An addictive mixture of sugar and fat, and a cup of strong tea. At midnight, I fall asleep. Then I'm awakened by the beam of a flashlight. . . .

541 I jump out of bed. There's someone with a flash-light just behind the garage door. It's one in the morning, the curfew in full force.

542 There are abductions practically every day in 2005. For political, sectarian, or simply financial reasons. And they don't end well.

543 My cousin Mahomed had been clear. "If someone shows up after curfew, it's either the police or the militia."

544 The AK-47 is leaning against the wall, barrel pointed at the ceiling. If I pick it up, the risk of firing it or being fired upon is a lot higher.

545 I would rather leave it there. It's always better to use words. After all, I don't know who is there or the reason for their visit.

546 But what if it's someone from the militia disguised as a police officer and looking for cash? Someone who knows that I have a dual nationality and comes looking for a Frenchman?

547 I decide to go outside without the Kalashnikov. In Iraq, this kind of situation should be taken seriously. I walk into the garage.

548 The beam of the flashlight is bouncing up and down. My heart beats faster when I hear my name: "Feurat! Feurat! It's me!"

549 It's Mohamed's sullen friend. The 286-pound giant. He must have moved into my uncle's little shack without letting me know.

550 Him: "Feurat, can I have a little gasoline, please? The generator is empty!" Looks like I won't be abducted this evening, after all.

551 The power generator, the generating unit. How can you talk about Iraq without mentioning those? You can find them humming on every street corner.

552 Bombings by the Americans in 2003 had hit the country's important infrastructures. Bridges, factories, power stations.

553 There is, on average, only three hours of electricity per day in Iraq. It's provided by "al-Wataniya"—"the National" (electric service). The rest of the time you need to use a generator.

554 A thriving business. There are small and large generators. With the small ones, you can't run the refrigerator and the air-conditioning.

555 Most homes have a small generator that's made in China and used primarily to run the television and the fan.

556 You have to pull the cord hard to get it running. It sounds like a moped. Five liters of gas will get you through the day.

557 There's a new line of work in Iraq, thanks to both opportunity and initiative: the amp salesman. Each district has its own little electric company.

558 The amp salesman is the owner of an enormous grouping of generators in a small prefab. He spends the day there and sometimes even sleeps there.

559 Neighborhood residents have monthly subscriptions. They're charged by the ampere—fifteen dollars. A mid-sized house uses five amps a day.

560 An electrical wire is run from the generator to the house of each subscriber, sometimes over a distance of 500 meters. In Iraq, the electrical wire is king.

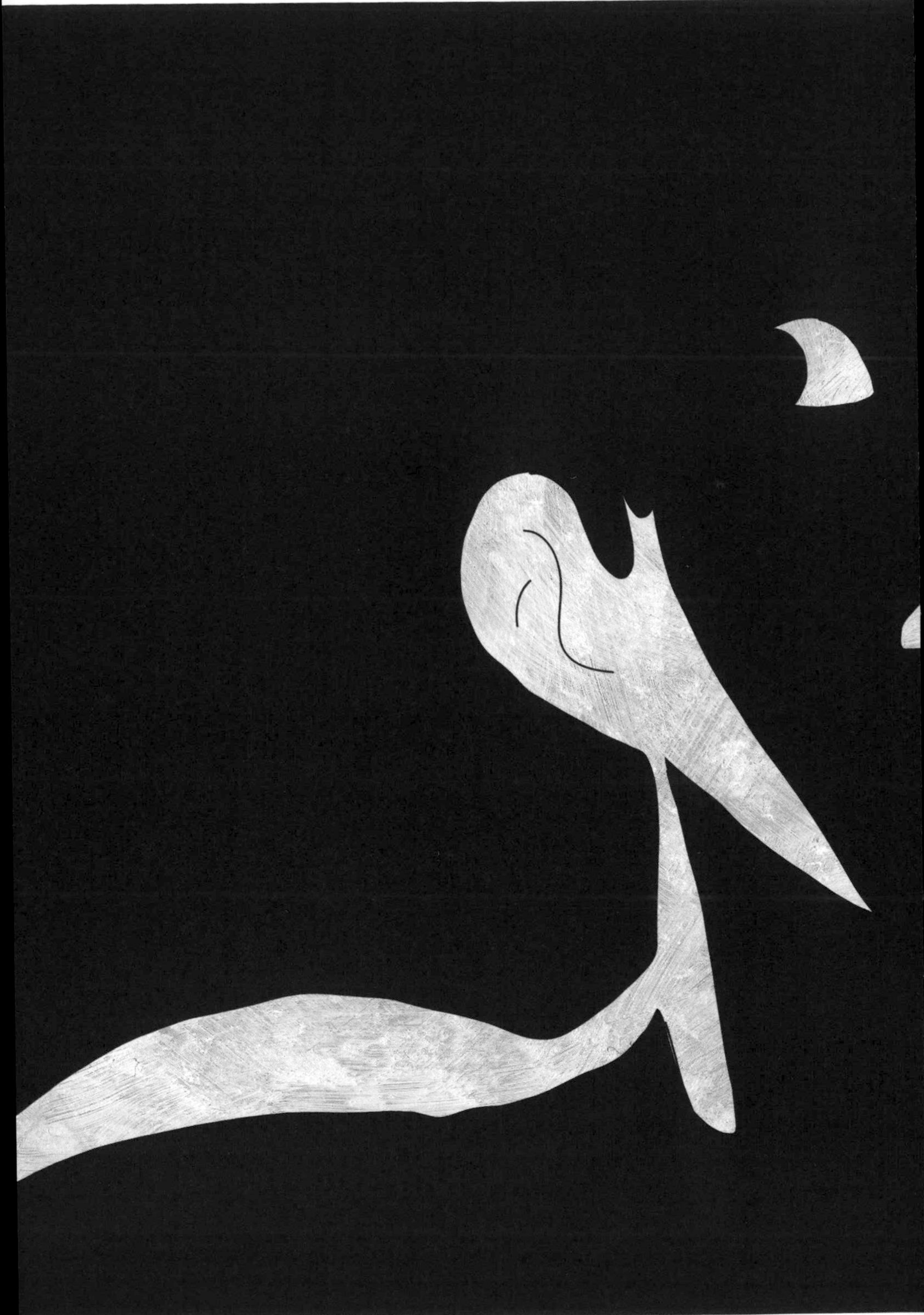

561 *Chai.* Iraqi tea is strong, almost black. It's served in an *istikan,* a small decorative glass for tea. It's very sweet, with cardamom.

562 Tea is an integral part of life in Iraq. It's part of the social fabric of the region and is drunk in the street and at home, in winter and in summer, in restaurants and in greasy spoons.

563 The fragrance of tea can resolve arguments. Cardamom calms the soul, tempers passions. It makes you forget the war.

564 It's served at home at least four times a day. At breakfast and at dinner. Never mind that it keeps you up at night.

565 Some drink it the traditional way. When it's too hot, you pour a little in the saucer to cool it down. And you sip it.

566 You make a lot of noise with your mouth when you drink *chai.* Having tea is like a musical composition punctuated by the whistle of the kettle. Misophonics beware.

567 Everyone drinks in his or her own way. Some by small, silent mouthfuls. Others in shots. Sometimes with two hands.

568 The sheik is obliged to dramatically slurp his mouthfuls of tea. This is how he establishes his presence, his authority.

569 The expression "Would you like a cup of tea?" doesn't exist in Iraq. You would never ask that. You serve tea as a matter of course.

570 Brought into Iraq by South Asians and their British occupiers, *chai,* which they called *East Tea Can,* morphed into *istikan* in Iraqi usage.

571 When I leave my house in Mansour each morning, I always have the feeling that I'm being watched. By neighbors and passersby.

572 A bizarre sensation that feels like something between a hunch and paranoia. It's as if the entire neighborhood knows. Knows what? That I'm French, and a journalist.

Georges Malbrunot
Christian Chesnot
Florence Aubenas
French journalists
abducted in Iraq in
2004 and 2005.

573 It's not a good thing to live alone and to be a #journalist, and it's even worse to be a French journalist in Baghdad. The proof: Georges Malbrunot and Christian Chesnot.

574 And then Florence Aubenas. What if that happened to me? Would my Iraqi passport save me from such a fate?

575 Iraqis are kidnapped every day for a pittance. Abduction. A thriving new business, just like generators.

576 A new shop called Sayed Halib opened up across the street. You can find anything there, from pajamas to spices.

577 Gone are the cries of street sellers. Nowadays, the sellers record their messages in advance, and a crackling loudspeaker does their work for them.

578 Some of these messages are inescapable. At the town market: "500 dinars, everything for 500 dinars!" Makes you wish you had earplugs.

579 This feeling of being watched comes over me every time I leave the house, and every time I return. Especially from the house next door.

580 Later I will learn that my cousin Mohamed asked my neighbors to surveil me. The sullen guy with the flashlight, for instance. . . .

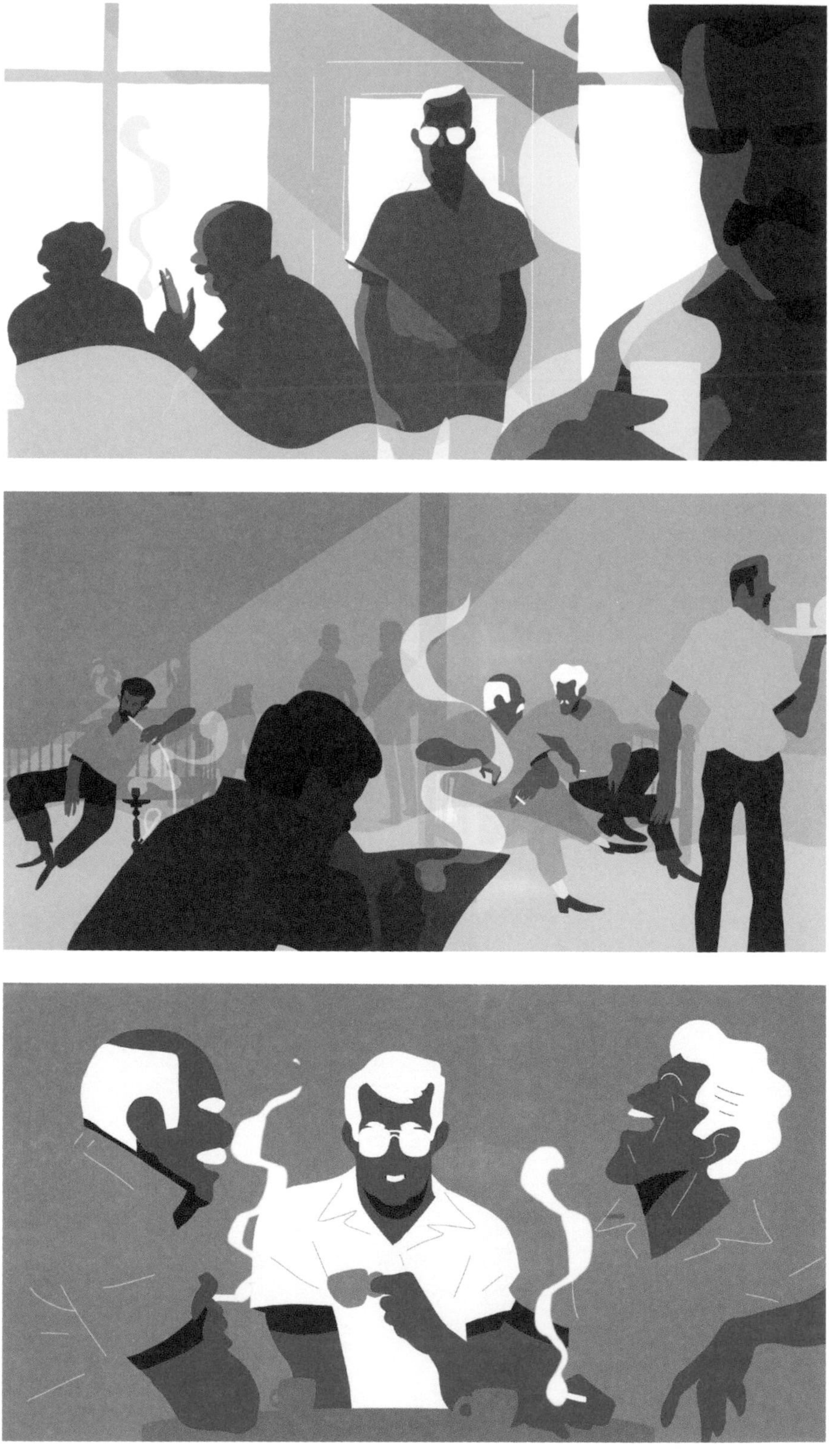

581 Each day, dozens of people die in Iraq. Bombings, murders, kidnappings, blunders on the part of mercenaries or American soldiers.

582 But on August 31, 2005, a simple rumor will lead to the death of almost 1,000 Iraqi pilgrims in less than one hour. On the al-Aima bridge.

583 The al-Aima bridge links two large historic districts of the capital: Kadhimiya and Adhamiya. The first Shiite, the second Sunni.

584 The Shia procession was heading to the shrine of Imam Musa al-Kadhim, the seventh Shiite imam. It wasn't a bomb or gunfire that killed them. It was just a rumor.

585 "There are suicide bombers in the crowd." The false rumor creates a wave of panic. Trampled and drowned, hundreds of pilgrims lose their lives.

586 Stressed by the panicked crowd, the bridge railing gives way. Death toll: 965. The bloodiest day since 2003.

587 The image circulates throughout the world: a sea of abandoned shoes on the al-Aima bridge. The Tigris River is an open-air grave.

588 During this tragedy, an unexpected event will calm the already growing (and exploited) tensions between the Shia and the Sunni.

589 Othman, a young Sunni swimming champion, rescues dozens of pilgrims before he drowns from exhaustion. A symbol of unity. And of the street.

590 A few years later, I'll meet Othman's father while directing a documentary, an Iraqi travelogue from the north of Iraq to the south.

591 The Karrada district in Baghdad is the place for outings to cafés, restaurants, boutiques, markets. It's the old, vibrant part of Baghdad.

592 That day, I go with my cousin Firas to Karrada. With his childhood friend Faisal, he had just opened a restaurant, al-Shmeisani.

593 Chicken along the lines of KFC. Wooden décor like in a mountain chalet. Dining terrace for at least fifty guests, and cooks from Bangladesh.

594 Faisal is a member of one of the large business families in Baghdad, and he lives in the house next door to the restaurant. He speaks slowly, like all his brothers.

595 Karrada is one of my favorite districts. Considered to be one of the town centers of the capital, it's not far from the seat of government.

596 Which makes this neighborhood an appealing target for car bombs. Not a week goes by without a huge explosion near a public building.

597 The police are everywhere. There are roadblocks on every street corner. And yet, a lot gets past them. Why? Because of a little device.

598 Used by the police, it's supposed to detect explosives. It resembles a little handgun with an antenna that looks like a barrel.

599 If the antenna points to a car, that car is stopped. "Do you have a weapon?" Oftentimes, a "no" will easily get you past the checkpoint.

600 The problem: these devices don't work. The British maker was sued for fraud. And it's the Iraqis who suffered.

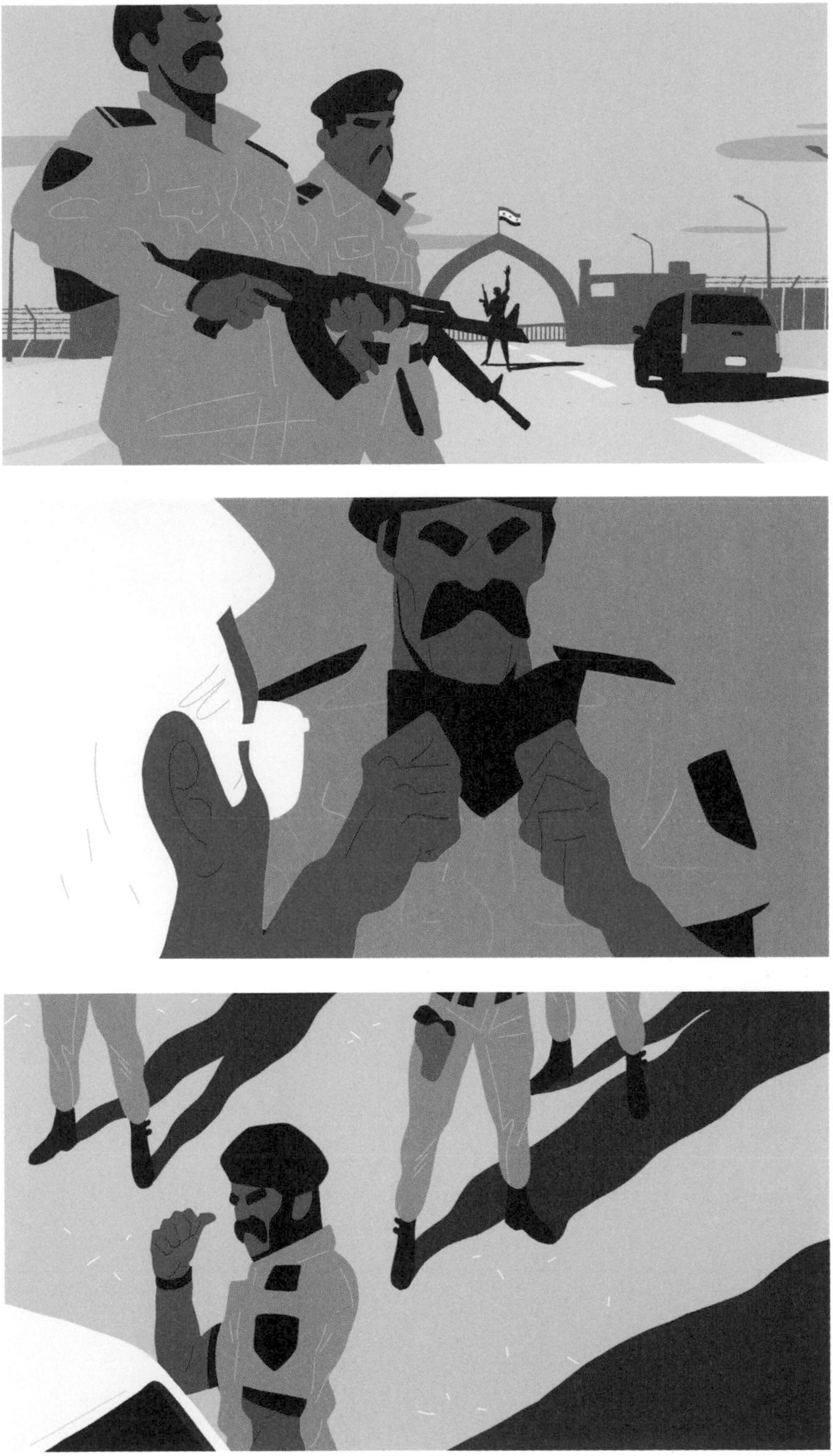

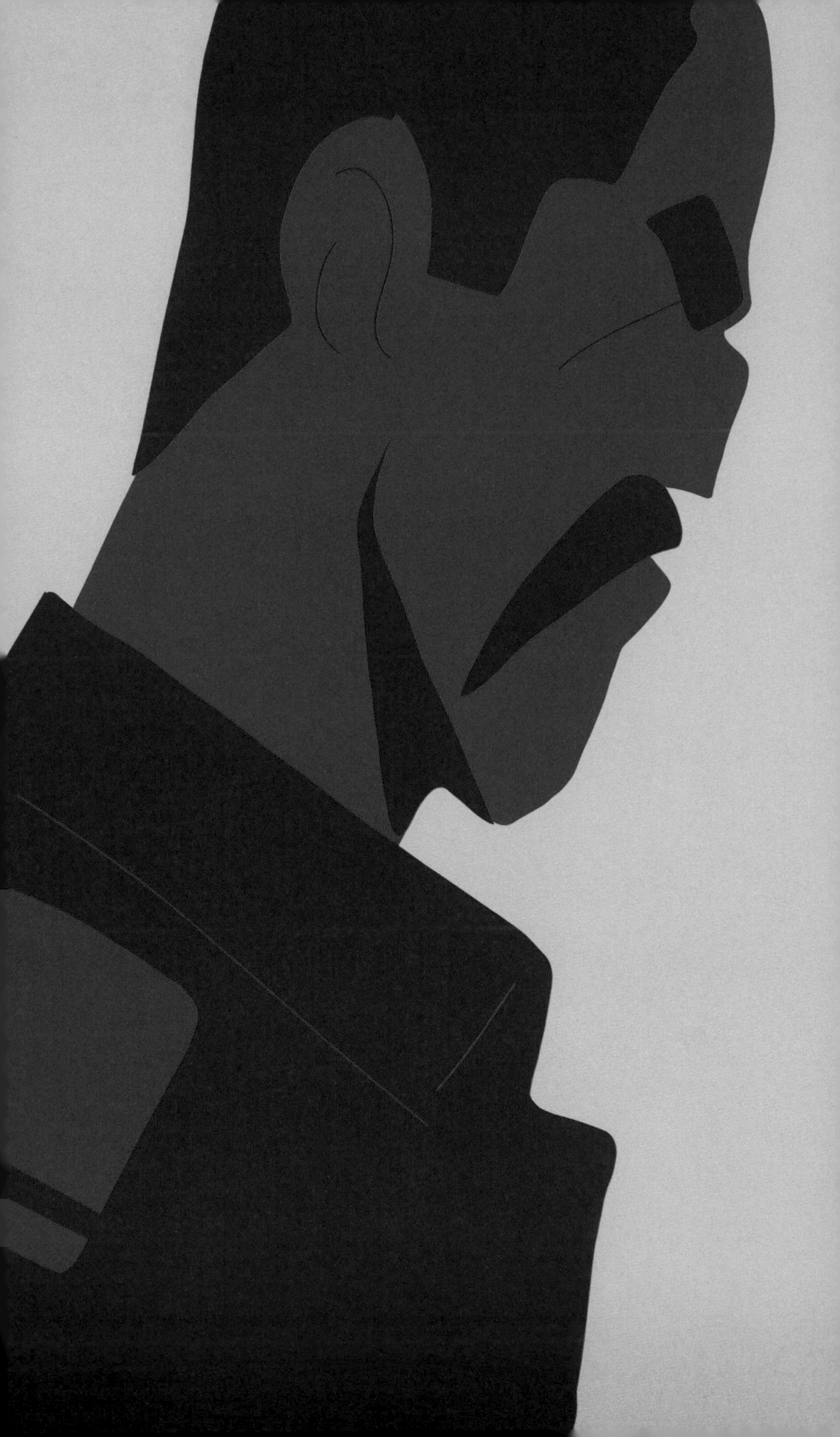

2005–2006 **I often hang out at the neighborhood barbershop. It's the ideal place to hear the latest news and rumors.**

601 The other problem in Iraq: the police. Ever since the arrival of "emperor" Paul Bremer and his efforts to dismantle Iraqi institutions, just about anyone could be recruited into the police.

602 Bakers, mechanics, and even the odd criminal who had spent time behind bars joined the police. They had to fill the void caused by Bremer.

603 My cousins told me about the long lines in police stations just after the fall of Baghdad on April 9, 2003. To pick up uniforms.

604 Recruiting wasn't a controlled process, and investigation was lacking when it came to each candidate's profile. There was no time for that. They needed them in droves.

605 To get around in Baghdad, I have two passports—French and Iraqi. I also have an unofficial press pass. Just in case.

606 But it's the fake press pass that I typically pull out at checkpoints. A photo, a stamp. The indispensable open sesame.

607 More often than not, what my cousins have told me is confirmed: The police at control points often don't know how to read. . . .

608 Sometimes, the policeman, his cap too big for his head, holds my card upside-down, looking uncomfortable before handing back my pass with a "yallah rooh!"—"Hurry up, get going!"

609 This lack of experience erodes trust. No one respects the law. You just need to get behind the wheel in Baghdad to understand that.

610 One day, I forget to stop at a checkpoint. The policeman yells: "If I were an American you would be arrested!" I didn't know how to respond to that.

611 There's a sandstorm today—something that occurs frequently in the summer. These storms usher in heavy clouds of red sand and whisk away the sounds of the city.

612 Slowly, the immense storm rolls in and devours Baghdad. Swallows up the entire city. Smothers all sounds of life.

613 In Mansour, Mazen comes to see me. We are outside in the garden when the enormous wall of sand bears down on us. Hussein, the gardener, puts down his rake.

614 It's the Americans' fault, explains Mazen. When they invaded Iraq, the army cut down an insane number of date palms, which had functioned quite effectively as bulwarks against the sand storms.

615 Consequently, life changed in some ways. First, there's no fighting on storm days. Sometimes you go four days without a sound.

616 Getting around is practically impossible. The suffocating heat ruins the asphalt. Asthmatics end up in the hospital, if they can get there.

617 Mazen and I are stuck. There's almost nothing in the house to eat. Visibility in the street is less than two meters.

618 There's a pizza that's more or less frozen, thanks to the outages. It's way past the expiration date on the box. No big deal.

619 That day, it's noon when the sky turns orange, almost red. The storm stops time. Stops the bombs. A rare moment of peace.

620 A moment of peace that will last four days. Once the sky is clear, life in Iraq resumes, with all its noise, its prayers, its drama.

621 2006 gets off to a bad start in Samarra, a town where Sunnis and Shia "coexist." Pretty much like the rest of Iraq.

The Askari Shrine of Samarra
حرم عسكريين
Holds the tombs of Ali al-Hadi and Hassan al-Askari, both Shiite. It is one of Shiite Islam's holiest sites.

622 On the horrific day of February 22, a bomb blows up the #GoldenDomeShrine of imams Ali al-Hadi and Hassan al-Askari. Claiming responsibility: al-Qaeda in Iraq.

623 No civilians are killed in the explosion, but the damage to the edifice is significant. The golden dome collapses—the symbolic collapse of Shiism.

624 If tension between Sunni and Shiite groups exists, this time it changes history just like September 11 did in the United States. A turning point.

625 I'm in Paris when the news breaks. My parents are worried. My father has a bad feeling: sectarian war has begun.

626 Hardly two hours after the attack, Shiite militants set fire to Sunni mosques and their worshippers. The monster is unleashed.

627 If 1995 was the dark year of the embargo, 2006 will be the darkest year after the war. The shock waves will be felt throughout the entire Middle East.

628 I'm on the next flight to Iraq, and circling down once more like a falling leaf over the Baghdad airport. I'm struck by the stony demeanor of the customs officials.

629 The road of death is calm. A few new craters. Mortal shells. I arrive in Amiriya. The district is closed off by the American army.

630 Amiriya has been attacked by the Muqtada al-Sadr militia—the #MahdiArmy. They formed neighborhood militias to defend themselves. There's no more talking. Only killing.

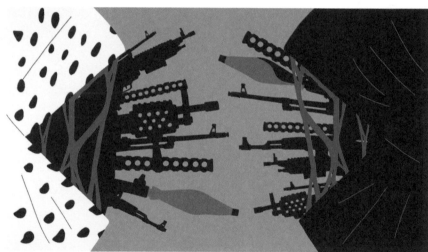

Mahdi Army
جيش المهدي
Militia of the
radical Shiite imam
Muqtada al-Sadr,
named for the large
Shia neighborhood
(Sadr City) in north-
east Baghdad.

631 I notice more and more religious paraphernalia in Amiriya. All talk is about the Mahdi Army, the militia led by the cleric in the black turban.

632 The Mahdi Army regularly pounds the area with mortal shells. The Sunni militia retaliates by expelling the Shiites.

633 Now there are empty homes. They're sometimes used by small factions. But they're frequently used by ordinary people.

634 I often hang out at the neighborhood barbershop. It's the ideal place to hear the latest news and rumors. Which are never good. . . .

635 The guy who cuts my hair speaks quietly, like he's confiding in me. "Do you know that they kill us now if we do threading?"

636 Threading. A traditional method of facial hair removal. You pinch the hair between two threads and pull to remove it.

637 The radicals who surveil the rest of us think that threading is too feminine. They make threats. And then they kill you if you don't cooperate.

638 Behind me there's another room closed off by a curtain. The barber murmurs. "We can thread you if you want. But not in the open." "No, thank you."

639 Crazy rumors are circulating as well. They'll kill anyone who mixes cucumbers and tomatoes in their market stalls. . . . I can't understand it.

640 The ice blocks some merchants sell in the streets? Banned. "A modern, unnatural invention," according to others (who nonetheless use cell phones). . . .

641   I take a walk with Mazen on Amiriya's main street in Baghdad. We drink *chai*. It's a rare moment of peace.

642   Black tea costs 250 dinars. With the devaluation, that comes to about 20 euro cents. To maintain respectability, you have to drink two.

643   In the midst of all the mouth noises and cigarette smoke, a black BMW slowly approaches the terrace. A window rolls down. . . .

644   A hand appears, holding a 9 mm pistol. A shot is fired. It's mayhem. We all run inside the restaurant, about twenty of us.

645   The emptied street reveals a man on the ground. No one goes up to him. "He was surely a traitor," exclaims one of the onlookers.

646   The car takes off in a squeal of tires. There's a police checkpoint only about sixty meters from here. In Iraq, they kill right under their noses.

647   The dead body of a "traitor" can remain on the street for one or two days. Sometimes a note on the back or torso explains why he was killed.

648   I hear in the neighborhood that garbage collectors are also targets. That's why the trash is piling up in the streets.

649   The reason? Groups put IEDs in the trash cans. When an American or Iraqi convoy drives by, the bomb is set off by cell phone.

650   The latest horror is to fill the dead bodies of animals with TNT. They often use street dogs for this. And there are a lot of them. . . .

651 We have our moments of extreme fear, and we have our moments of joy. We also have date season. Iraq was once the top world exporter of dates.

652 The Sumerians cultivated date palms more than 7,000 years ago, giving rise to the system of irrigation in Mesopotamia, which is now Iraq.

653 I discovered dates during the embargo. They were a replacement for chocolate at the time, and so my sister and I initially hated them.

654 But my father taught me that, like the 350-some types of cheese in France, there were just as many varieties of dates in Iraq.

655 My favorite is the *hillawi*, a yellow-brown date that is crunchy and honey-like. It's typically harvested at the end of summer, in September.

656 The best ones come from Basra, or the "Venice of the Middle East," as it was once called. The palm groves in southern Iraq are now wastelands.

657 The date palm is similar to humans in that there are male trees and female trees. Hand pollination helps to establish palm groves.

658 My father has spoken about a very rare variety that bears fruit only every three or four years. It's a very dark blue date.

659 I have yet to find this blue date. With the war, date production in Iraq has slowed down. Palm groves have disappeared.

660 In Iraq, dates are traditionally eaten with fermented yogurt. This strange dish is a delicacy for the poor. Deliciously decadent.

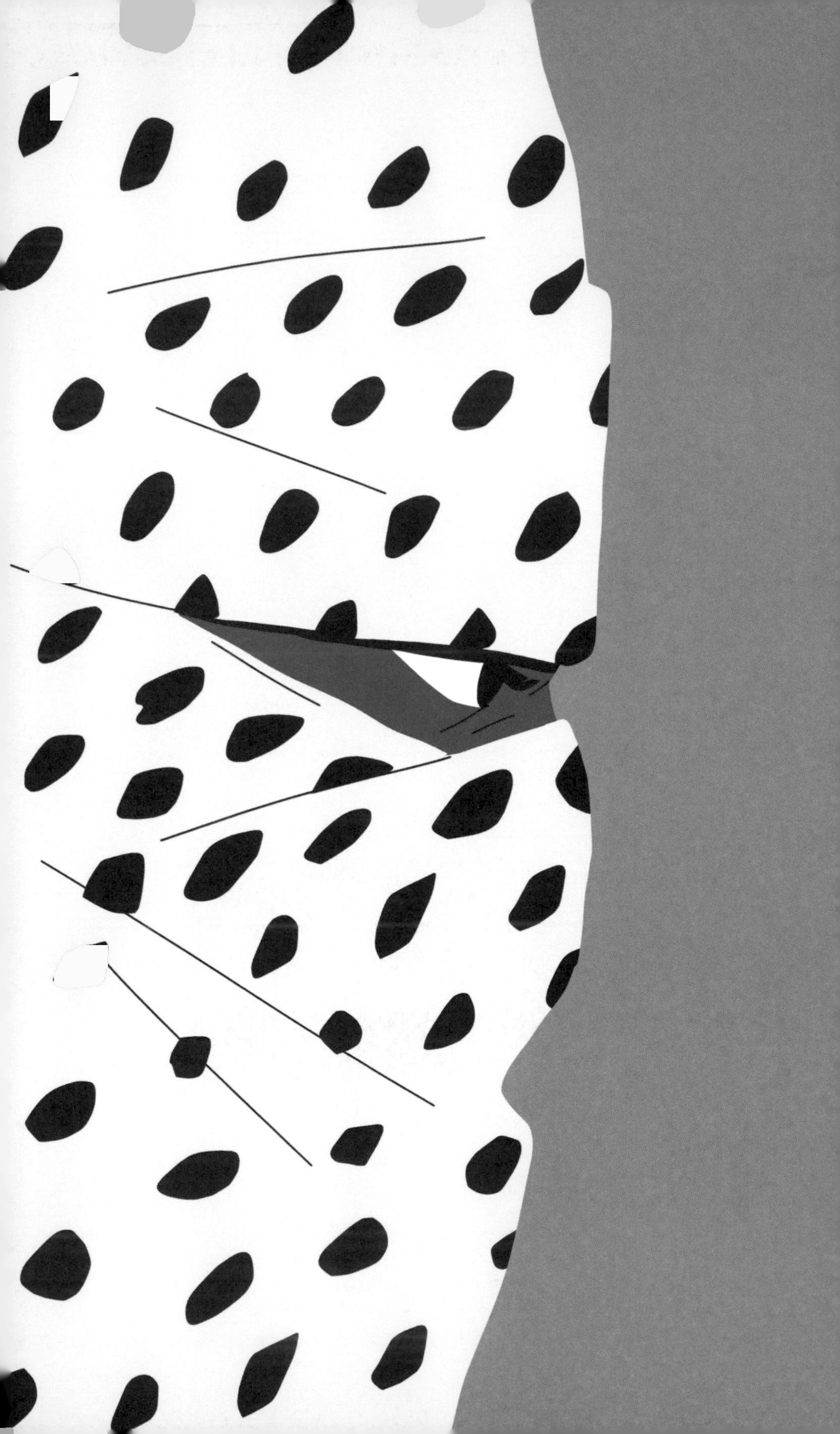

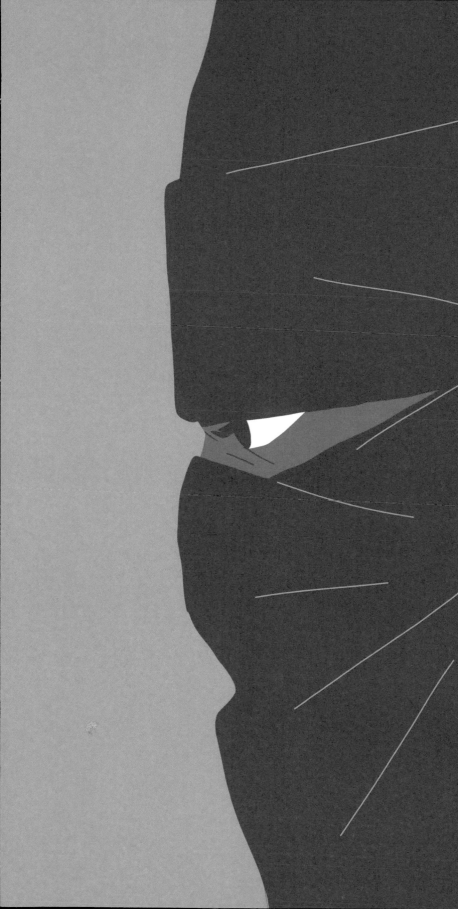

661 It's the start of a war between Sunni and Shia militias. On one side, the militias of the Mahdi Army and related groups. On the other, al-Qaeda and related groups.

662 Each day, you can find about 100 dead bodies in the streets of Baghdad and elsewhere. Very often handcuffed. Tortured. Executed.

663 Sometimes people die because they have the wrong first name—"Omar" or "Hussein." It's as simple as that. The deadly power of the symbolic.

664 A new business is born. Fabricating fake ID cards. In 2006, most young Iraqi men have two different ID cards. One with a Sunni name. The other Shiite.

665 During a check or an abduction, you hope to take out the right card, based on the uniform in front of you or the accent. Or foresight.

666 One sunny day in the streets of Karrada, I'm photographing an arrest—a stupid thing to do in 2006. The policeman sees me and questions me.

667 I have the wrong passport with me. The Iraqi one with my last name that is common in al-Anbar. He accuses me of being a terrorist. "Erhabi!"

668 He raises his Kalashnikov. Threatens to kill me. I'm detained, handcuffed to a young thug from Ramadi, the one who was arrested earlier.

669 He insults us. For several hours, I find myself in the shoes of a "Sunni" persecuted by a member of the Shia militia disguised as a police officer.

670 "I'm going to kill you." The veins in his temples are bulging. There is hatred in his eyes. Fear also. I really think this is the end for me.

671 The militia-policeman watches me in the rear-view mirror. "If I see my face in one of your photos, I'll kill you on the spot."

672 He's convinced. "You took my photo because you're al-Qaeda." No matter what I said, he wouldn't believe me. My name was enough.

673 I tell him I'm a French reporter. He doesn't believe me, because in 2006, western journalists don't dare to step outside their secure hotels. His forehead is beaded with sweat.

674 The Ramadi guy I'm cuffed to remains silent. He smiles stupidly. The policeman continues to insult me, sometimes waving around his AK-47.

675 He picks up my camera. Fortunately, the batteries are dead. He can't verify whether I'd taken his photo or not. That's a bit of a relief.

676 I have other photos on this camera. There are armed men. A car riddled with bullets. Photos I took while researching a story.

677 If he sees them, he'll absolutely believe his version of the story. What a mess. I thought I was shielded but I'm just another Iraqi here.

678 Maybe the word "journalist" gave him pause. He decides to take me to the station to consult with the chief.

679 I spend four hours in the Karrada police station. I see people getting slapped around. And I'm there simply because I took an unauthorized photo.

680 They allow me a phone call. I ask my cousin Mazen to bring my French passport. The police chief lectures me.

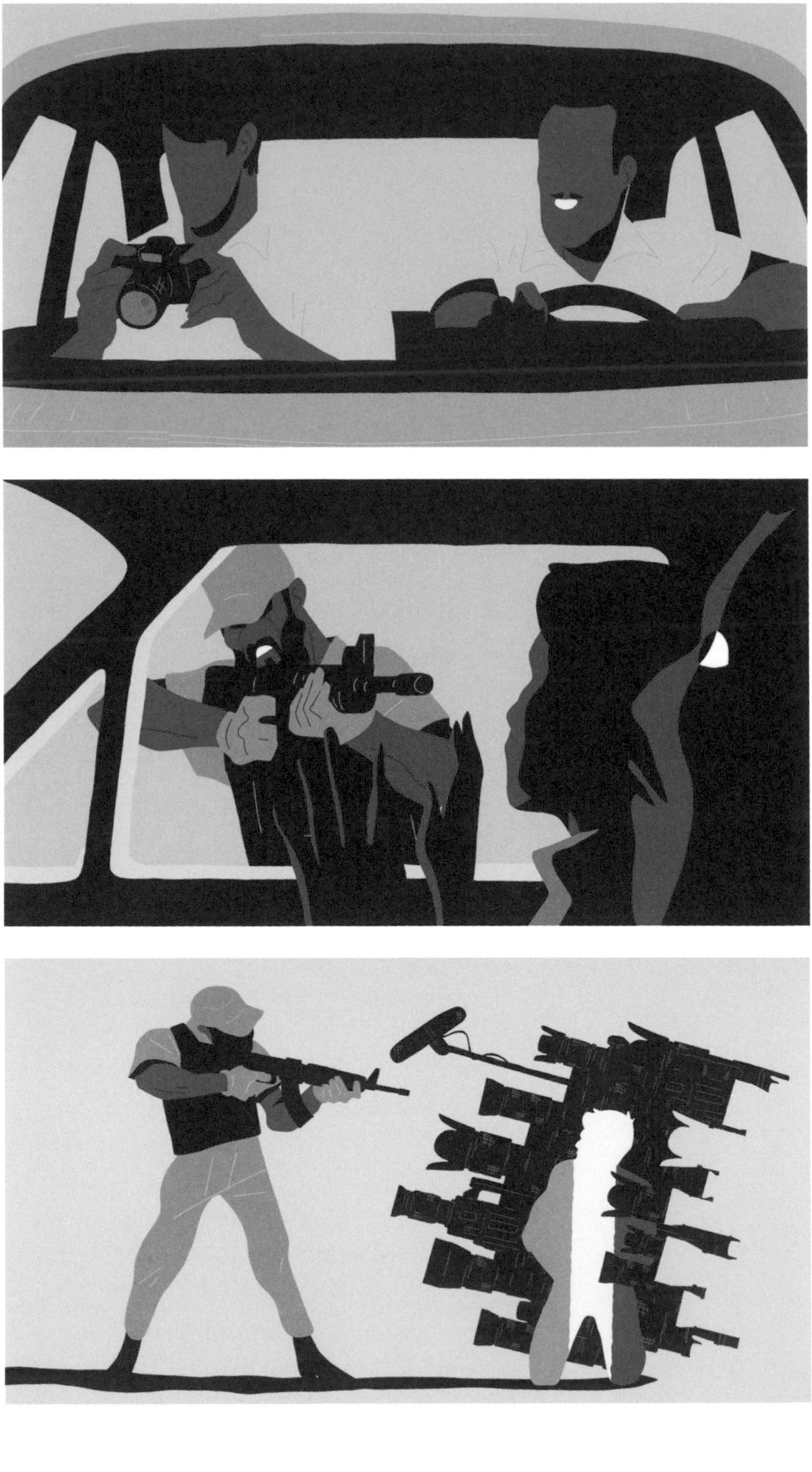

681 Having believed for one long hour that the militia-policeman was going to kill me in Karrada, I can now breathe a little more easily. I think I'll get through this.

682 My camera is at the station. No one has batteries to check the photos. They decide to let me leave.

683 Better to steer clear of the police station. I go back to Amiriya for a few more days before returning to France. But the nightmare isn't over.

684 Not long after my return to France, a large-scale military operation would be launched by the Americans in Amiriya, which had become a stronghold for a number of Iraqi armed groups.

685 But now in Mansour, the neighborhood is on lockdown. We can't go out without the risk of being arrested by the Americans. If you're young, you're suspicious.

686 At the wheel of Mazen's BMW, I'm driving along the main thoroughfare at dusk, when it's hard to tell a dog from a wolf.

687 Mazen yells "Stop!" In front of us, a green laser is sweeping the street. An American sniper tells us to turn around. With his gun.

688 We return empty-handed, without dinner. It's better to stay inside and lock the door. But some evenings, you're not so lucky.

689 "Open the door, motherfucker!" The door has no choice—it's kicked open. Our neighbor has been the target of an American military intervention squad.

690 At the time, I'm in the kitchen. On my left, a window looks out over the front entrance. I turn my head. A full-face helmet is looking my way.

691 It's an American soldier who is securing the area while my neighbor is raided. He looks at me, motionless.

692 I'm alone in front of the refrigerator, which doesn't work without *al-Wataniya*, the national electric service. I proceed to open the refrigerator door.

693 A surreal moment. The green laser is moving around the kitchen, around me, and stops on the white fridge. The soldier is watching me closely.

694 My heart is beating out of my chest. And if he shot me as a precaution? I'm alone in a supposedly insurgent neighborhood. This won't make the news.

695 I act as naturally as I can in such surreal circumstances. I slowly reach for a bottle of water. It's not very cold, but I drink it anyway.

696 The laser is darting around me. I slowly put the bottle back into the refrigerator. I close the door and turn around in one fluid motion.

697 The seconds pass and seem interminable to me. I slowly leave the room with my hands at my sides and in a sweat. A stupid way to die. No.

698 The next day, news of the operation makes its way through the neighborhood. Mohamed F., a member of the Islamic Army in Iraq, was arrested.

699 Not to be confused with the Islamic State of Iraq. The Islamic Army in Iraq is composed of former officers and Islamists.

700 Very powerful, the group is organized and operating from Baghdad to Mosul. It's a propaganda machine, well before its time. Well before ISIS.

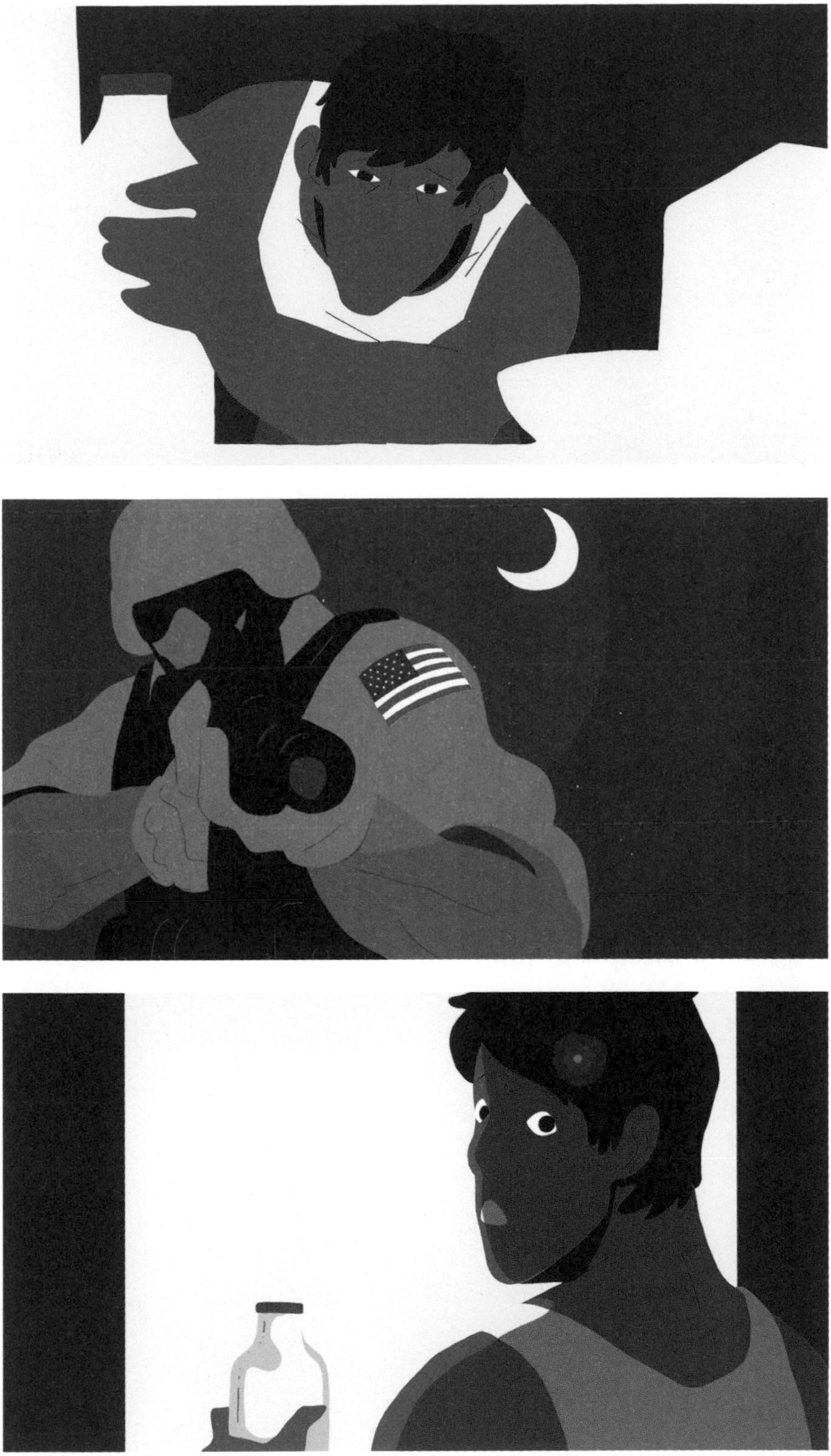

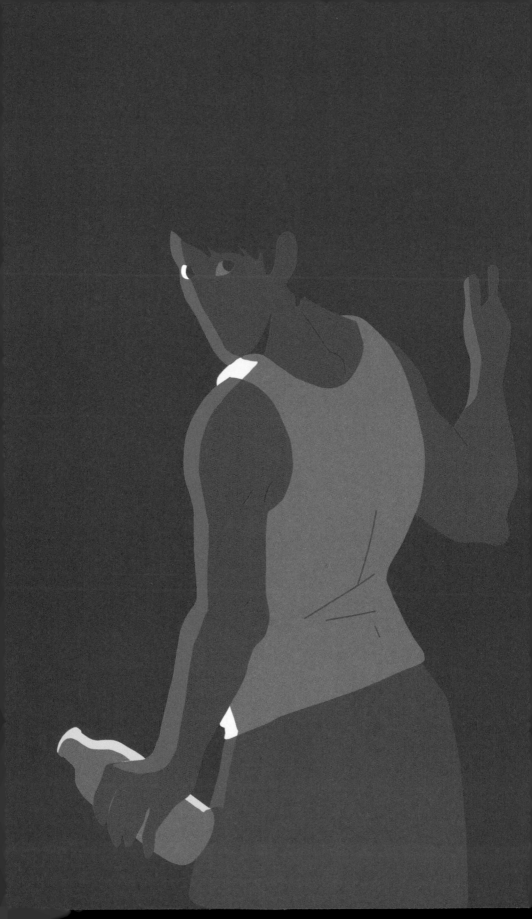

2006 **My Iraq is, above all, a bunch of smells. Sand, watermelon, *masgouf*, cardamom tea, sourdough rolls.**

701 It's been a tough week. First, I thought the militia was going to kill me. Then I was scoped out by the green laser on an American soldier's gun.

702 Amiriya is still locked down by the Americans. I can't go out. Mazen and I stay at home most of the time.

703 The streets are empty. Almost all the shops are closed. And another sandstorm is upon us. Amiriya. The scene of an apocalypse.

704 A bit of excitement happens on Friday, the day of prayer. I go to the mosque with Mazen. The streets are crowded, the imam is there.

705 People are tense. The imam is preaching with a solemn air. He knows the Americans are there with their Iraqi translators, listening.

706 The imam uses words that the Iraqi government can't stand: "occupation," "torture," "militias." He's sharing awful photos.

707 The dead bodies of Sunnis who were tortured by the militia in Basra and Mahdi. Some bodies have burn marks and drill holes. Sheer horror.

708 The imam finishes his prayer by saying he's received threats from the government. Worshippers offer to take him in, including Mazen. I'm an observer.

709 There's a crowd outside the mosque. Two masked men are distributing CD-ROMs. The worshippers grab them.

710 I get one. The title is *Qanass Bagdad*—*The Sniper of Baghdad*. I haven't yet heard of him. Or of the myth. I load the CD into my computer.

711   The title appears on the screen: *The Sniper of Bagh-dad*. Then there are *anasheed*—battle songs—followed by the first scene. An American soldier.

712   Graphic effects: A target mark appears on the soldier's head. A shot is fired. The image shakes. The soldier falls.

713   Second scene. A soldier looks bored in the turret of his battle tank. It could be in Ramadi or in Fallujah. Target. *Bang*. The soldier collapses.

714   I can't believe it. I'm watching soldiers die, one after the other. At least twenty of them. *Bang*. Dead.

715   Behind me are Mazen and a neighbor, their eyes wide. They're surprised but not as shocked as I am. The neighbor laughs at each "bang."

716   The video ends with a shot of a masked sniper. A "hero" named Juba. I don't understand his name. For me, Juba is the capital of South Sudan.

717   The sniper cleans his rifle before putting it down on a table. Then we see numbers. In 2006, Juba apparently killed 160 American soldiers.

718   On the screen is the logo of the Islamic Army in Iraq. These are the ones who kidnapped the two French journalists Malbrunot and Chesnot.

719   Whether Juba is a hero or a myth, the kills were all real. He was a notorious figure in Iraq and the US and was drawn by Brazilian political cartoonist Carlos Latuff.

720   I'm told these CDs were all the rage in the Arab world, from Cairo to Algiers. In Iraq, the hunt for the Sniper of Baghdad is underway. He's WANTED.

721　Mothballs. The smell of closets. The smell of suitcases. The smell of travels. Even before apricots, mothballs are my first olfactory memory of Iraq.

722　In 1989, when I opened the closet at my aunt Enaam's in my room in Yarmouk, I got a nose full of mothballs.

723　Mothballs, a smell I started to like when I would open my mother's suitcase to look for something, then close it, empty-handed.

724　Mothballs, the smell of sad departures, the heart-break of separation when I shook hands and kissed people goodbye in Baghdad.

725　Mothballs, the smell of being searched by the Jordanians at the Trebil border crossing. Sheepishly wiping away the tears. A heavy heart.

726　Mothballs, used for keeping moths away. Today, they revive old stories. Of travels. Of the road. Of a country. My country.

727　It's the only smell today that can make my heart ache, that can stop me in my tracks. Sometimes with a smile, and other times with a grimace.

728　Olfactory memory is the hardest kind to erase. It's the most emotional, the most arbitrary. It opens the door without knocking.

729　Mothballs, is this the smell of time? The symbiosis of an occasion from the past and the imagination? A moment of pain or pleasure?

730　My Iraq is, above all, a bunch of smells. Sand, watermelon, *masgouf*, cardamom tea, sourdough rolls. Mothballs.

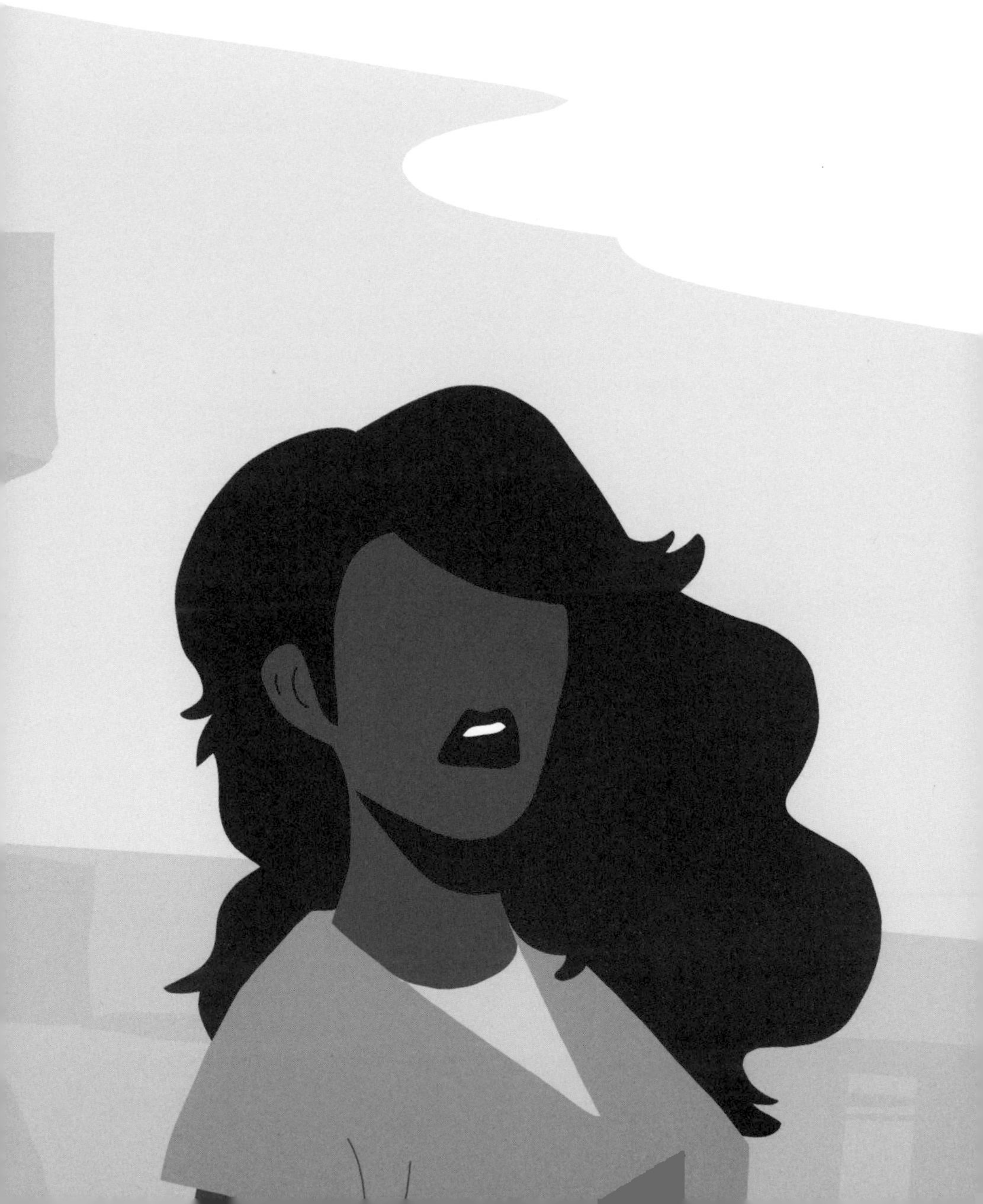

731 It's the end of 2006. Not much of my family on my mother's side remains in Baghdad. My cousin Taghreed still lives in the Yarmouk district.

732 Every morning, she faces the very real danger of going to work in the pharmacy that her husband and a friend run inside a hospital.

733 At the time, the Ministry of Health is under the direction of the Sadrist Movement, a political branch of Muqtada al-Sadr and his Mahdi Army.

734 A little like the Muslim Brotherhood in Egypt, the Sadrists control Shia networks and public agencies, like hospitals.

735 That week, I'm looking after Taghreed's children. A boy of 5 years and a girl of 8. School is closed—it's a missile target.

736 I spend time with them. We watch TV. They bicker. One morning, there's an explosion near the house, as is often the case.

737 As a reflex, the two kids jump down in front of the sofa. They explain that they learned this in school: get away from the windows as quickly as possible.

738 How do you do schoolwork in these conditions? What will the future be for Iraqi children? My little cousins have grown up with the sounds of war.

739 One evening, Taghreed's husband's friend stays for dinner with us. Ahmed A. is a redhead who was released from the Abu Ghraib prison not too long ago.

740 He says he's in the Salafi resistance. He doesn't fight but he helps out. Here's a paradox, though: He also works for the Ministry of Health.

741 When Ahmed A. sits down next to me, he wants to talk about only two things. The practice of Salafi Islam and the Baghdad resistance.

742 I listen to him closely and smile, when he suddenly stops speaking to ask me why I don't go to the mosque.

743 He continues on, saying the Salafi resistance is the best organized resistance in Baghdad. I'm surprised by his openness.

744 He doesn't fight, but he carries weapons in his car from point A to point B. He also tells me about the torture he experienced at Abu Ghraib.

745 Handcuffed to a wall for 24 hours, and very loud music that makes it impossible to sleep. Since his release, he has shaved his beard and wears jeans.

746 Ahmed A. understands that I'm an observer in this conflict rather than an actor. He stops proselytizing. He becomes a friend and a reliable source.

747 Ahmed A. represents just how complex Iraq has become after 2003. A (Salafi) public servant at the Ministry of Health under the control of the Sadrists.

748 My concern about how openly he spoke about his activities was well-founded. One evening, Ahmed receives a phone call. A trap. He steps right in it.

749 On the phone, they tell him that the Minister of Health wants to see him. "Tomorrow." Ahmed puts on a shirt. Starts up his white car.

750 They close in on him in the Ministry parking lot. Four members of the Mahdi Army beat him up and then put a bullet in his head.

751 In spite of objections from friends and family, I'm still walking around Baghdad alone, practically incognito.

752 The war between the Sunni and Shia militias is raging. You still see about 100 dead bodies in the streets and in the Tigris River every day.

753 Practically my entire family has left Baghdad for neighboring countries, like Jordan and Syria, or for more remote places like Canada and the US.

754 One day, I'm wandering around al-Tahrir Square, which is a little smaller than its equivalent in Cairo but just as central and symbolic.

755 Not too far away is the magnificent al-Rasheed Street, with its columns yellowed by time and the elements. Its scrap dealers and their weathered faces.

756 I walk up Sadoun Street to get to the famous Liberation Square. I'm looking for a place I can no longer find.

757 I ask a traffic cop for directions. Mistake. He finds that suspicious and looks me up and down, asking me if I'm from here.

758 Paranoid? Maybe he thinks I'm a suicide bomber. Walking around alone in Baghdad in 2006? It looks sketchy. I thank him and walk away.

759 He watches me and then starts talking into his phone. This time I'm the paranoid one. A car stops next to me.

760 Four men with mustaches look me over. They might be *Mukhabarat*. What's going on? What have I done wrong?

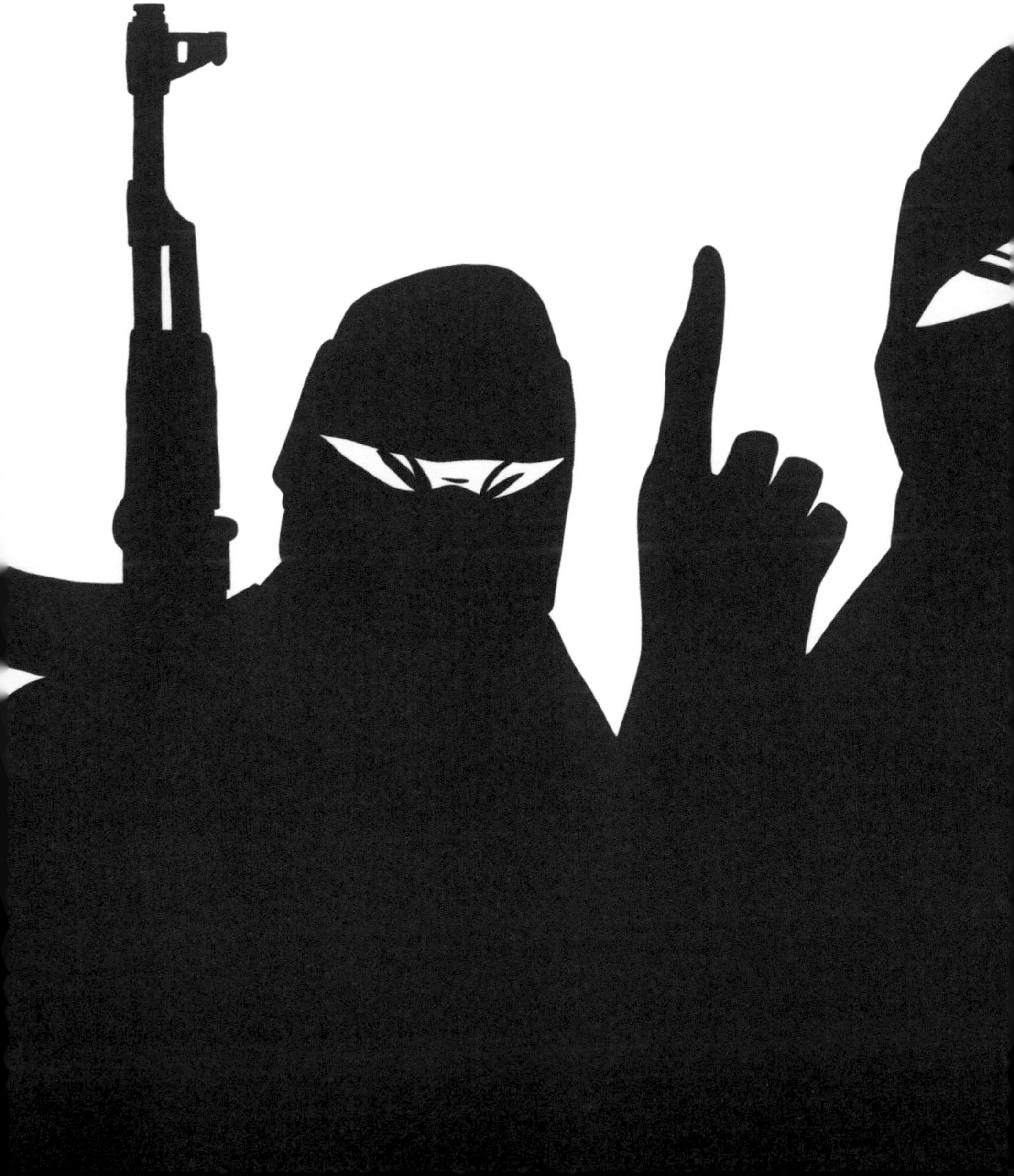

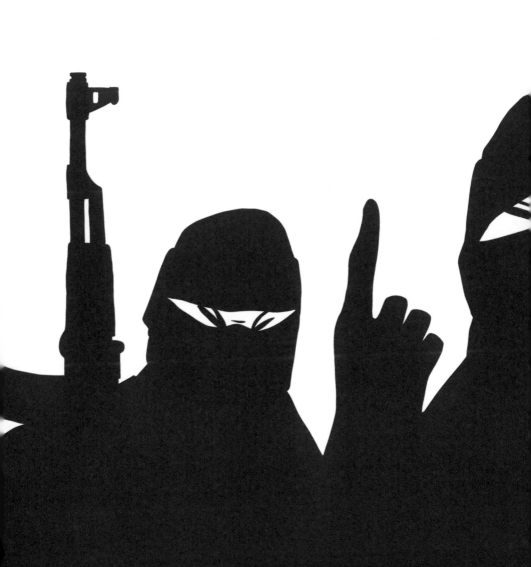

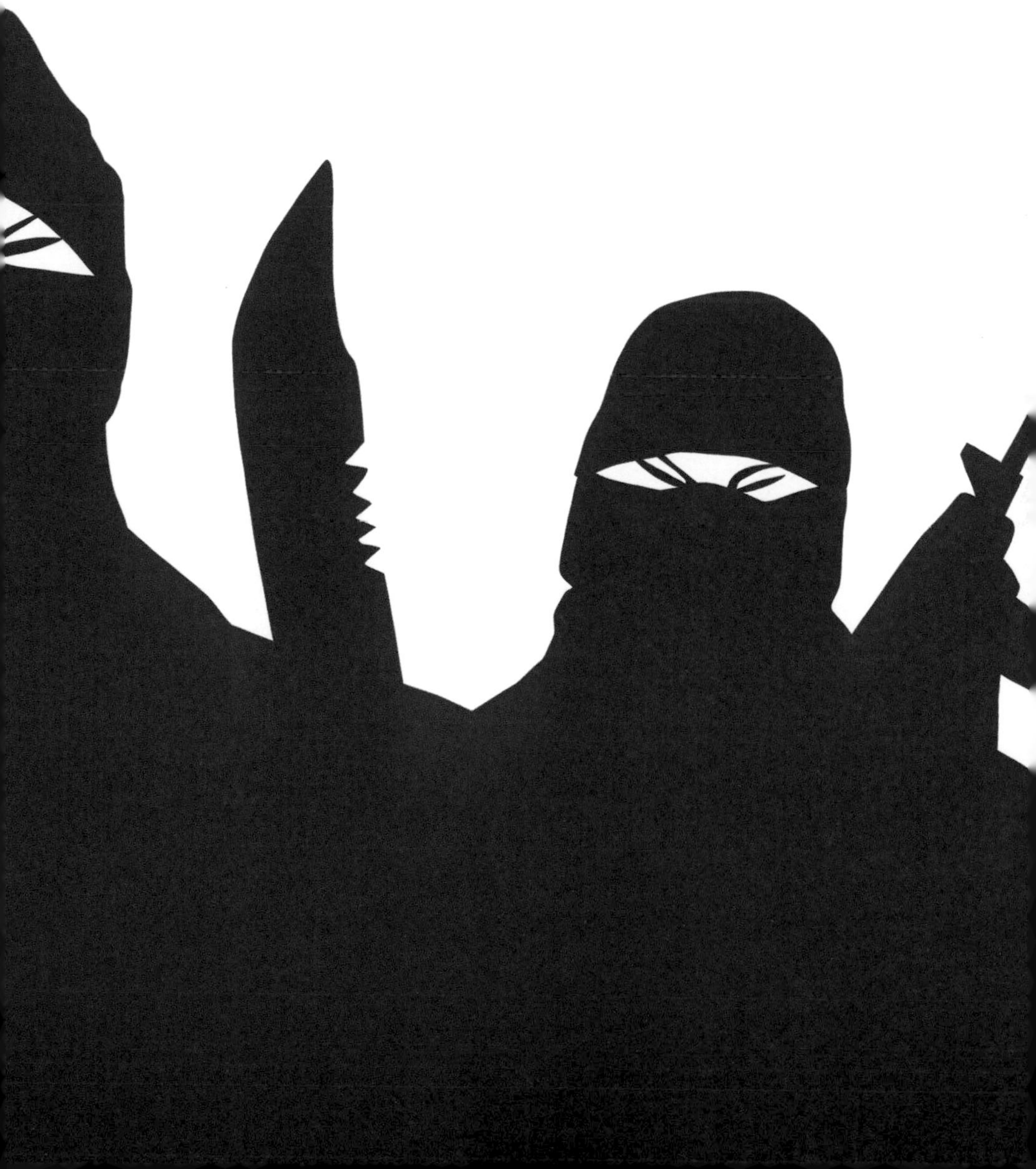

761 Paranoia gets the best of me. I take out my cell phone and call a cousin while keeping an eye on the mustaches. They are staring at me. The cop has left.

762 In Baghdad, things happen every day for different reasons: sectarian, political, or, most often, financial. It's an entire industry.

763 My cousin Abdelatif doesn't live too far from here. He takes my call, tells me not to move. Fifteen minutes go by. *Very. Slowly.*

764 I recognize his gray BMW. He picks me up at the roundabout, and we race off. I look back. The mustaches haven't moved.

765 I feel ridiculous and say so to Abdelatif. He answers in all seriousness that I'm not ridiculous. This is often how abductions happen.

766 Some kidnappers are very organized, and others just go after you. I was a target, according to Abdelatif. "It's the look," he said.

767 I speak the Iraqi dialect, but, according to Abdelatif, simple details can betray me. My walk, my clothes, my expression.

768 I'd rather be ridiculous than kidnapped. Instinct prevails. So does hunger. We get some food at Tea Time in the quiet district of Harthia.

769 Even in Baghdad in 2006, there are some districts where the war seems distant. In Harthia, all the fashionable restaurants are bustling with young people.

770 It's one of the few districts where you see groups of girls walking about, with or without veils, alone or accompanied. Like at university.

771　The situation becomes rather dangerous for me. I've been in Mansour for four months now. One day I'm French, the next I'm Iraqi.

772　The sectarian vibe is heavy. In Baghdad, the wrong first name, accent, article of clothing, the way you swear, can cost you your life.

773　I go to Jordan for a couple weeks. Half of my family on my mother's side lives there. But first, a short detour to Kurdistan.

Kurdistan Region of Iraq
Region of northern Iraq that has been autonomous since 1991. Its capital is Erbil and has a majority Kurdish population.

774　This is my first time in Erbil. The #Kurdistan Region of Iraq is another Iraq within Iraq. A peace haven. A new frontier and language.

775　"Shoni kaka? Bekherbe," says the mustached driver. "Mamnoun," I say. It's the only thing I know how to say. "Kurdi nazanem"—I don't speak Kurdish.

776　The citadel is the jewel in the crown of the capital of Iraqi Kurdistan. This ancient pre-Sumerian fortress overlooks the city.

777　In the streets downtown, I hear the Baghdadi dialect of those who have fled the capital to escape sectarian and American violence.

778　When you're an "Arab" Iraqi, you can't stay in Kurdistan unless you have a Kurdish guarantor. But I can get around that because I'm French.

779　Something I can't get around, however, is the interrogation by the asayesh, or Kurdish police. I'm from Fallujah, and that makes them nervous.

780　Them: "Why Erbil? And for how long?" My heart answers: Because it is also my country. But I show my credentials, smile, and nod my head.

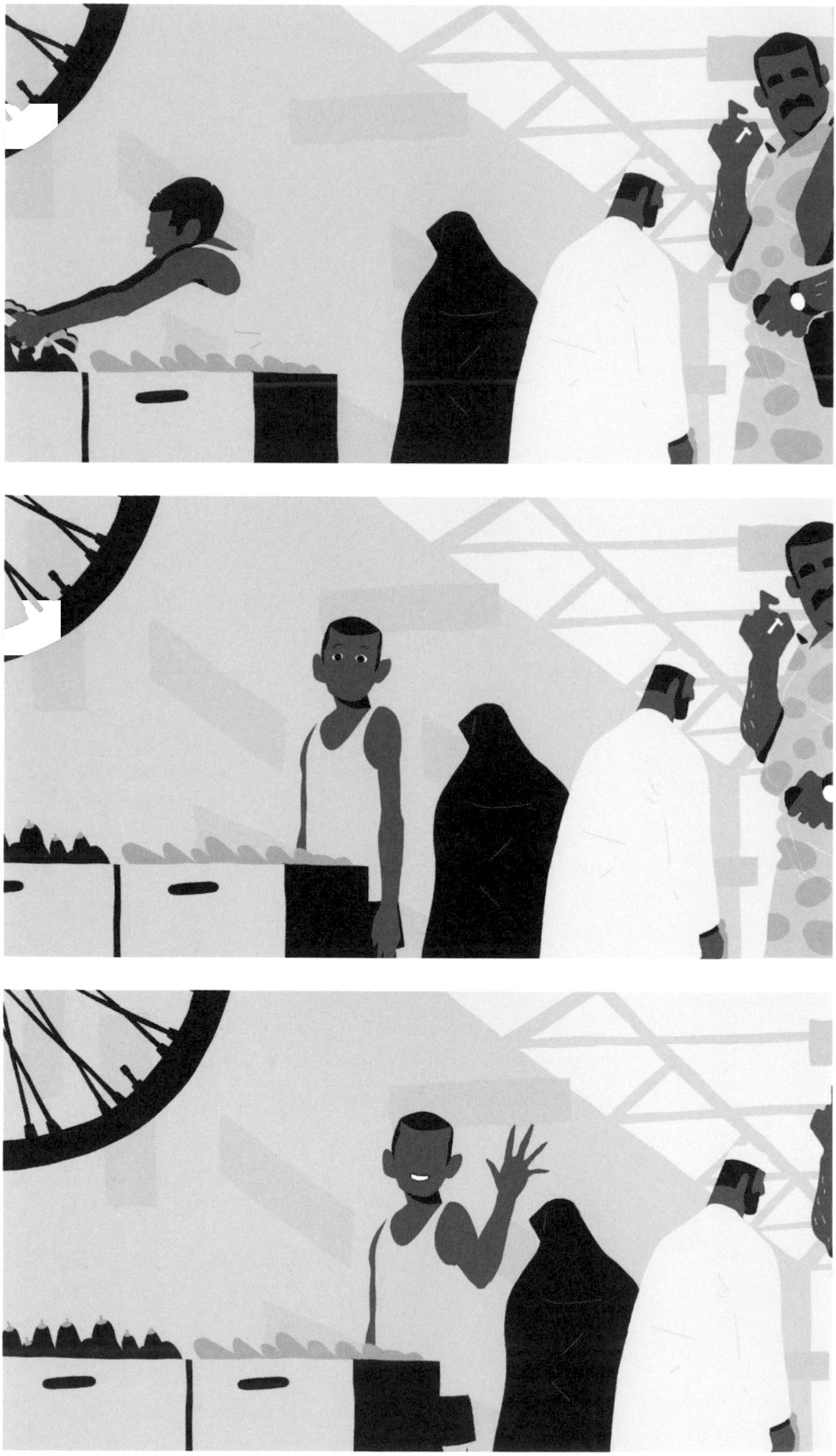

781 As I leave the offices of the *asayesh*, a police officer tells me that Fallujah is synonymous with terrorism for a lot of people here.

782 He's not wrong. Each time someone asks me where I'm from in Iraq, they joke "Erhabi?"— "Terrorist?"

783 But on the whole, I'm getting my bearings. The Kurds I meet are pleasant and welcoming. At the base of the citadel, the Mam Khalil Café.

Mustafa Barzani
مصطفى البارزاني
Kurdish leader and head of the 20th-century national Kurdish movement. He is the founder of the Kurdistan Democratic Party, and a symbol of the Kurdish cause.

784 Arabic music plays on a constant loop. On the walls are photos of #MustafaBarzani (Masoud's father). And photos of King Faisal II, overthrown in 1958.

785 Here the history of Iraq has the flavor of cardamom tea, the everlasting symbol of what unites Kurds and Arabs in this café.

786 On the terrace, the Kurdish flag hangs overhead. Arabic music in the background and conversations in Kurdish weave together like an Iraqi tapestry.

787 In the *souk*, you can see the Ottoman influence in the architecture and in the goods for sale. Up on the hill, the citadel is still a residential area.

788 But people who live there will soon be relocated. UNESCO wants to renovate and preserve the citadel's walls. Transform it into a tourist attraction.

789 Children play soccer in the narrow streets. The occasional foreign tourist takes photos. I meet an English professor from Poland.

790 In Baghdad, people dream of a peaceful haven like this one. Kurdistan is the region that fares the best during this Iraqi catastrophe. But at what price?

791 Two sisters, the same destiny: prison, escape, asylum. They came from Iranian Kurdistan, where they fought with the PJAK.

PKK
Kurdistan Workers' Party, formed in 1978. This armed group with Marxist tendencies is considered a terrorist group by much of the international community.

792 Its origins are of some dispute, but the PJAK has a lot in common with the rhetoric and methods of the PKK, whether it's an outgrowth of the PKK or not.

793 That day, the sisters invite me to a picnic at PJAK, which was established in Erbil in 2004. I am invited on a "press trip."

794 There are about twenty of us in the bus, including two American women, my Polish friend, and Iraqi Kurds among the rest. I'm the only Arab.

795 The two sisters speak Sorani and therefore have no trouble communicating with their Iraqi brothers. The latter look at them with devotion.

796 In the bus, the two Americans are talking about Ainkawa, the suburb of Erbil where the Chaldean refugees of Karakosh, Mosul, and elsewhere reside.

797 It's interesting to see them on a bus that's being driven by a far-left Kurdish independence group fighting against Iran.

798 Driving through mountains reminiscent of Switzerland, we stop at an altitude of 1,500 meters. On the menu: sandwiches and political discussion.

799 One of the leaders explains the reason for their battle with Iran—the reunification of Iraqi Kurds, Iranians, Syrians, and Turks. A pipe dream.

800 The discussion is over, and the two sisters start to dance under the foggy eye of the Qandil Mountains. And under the captivated gaze of their Iraqi brothers.

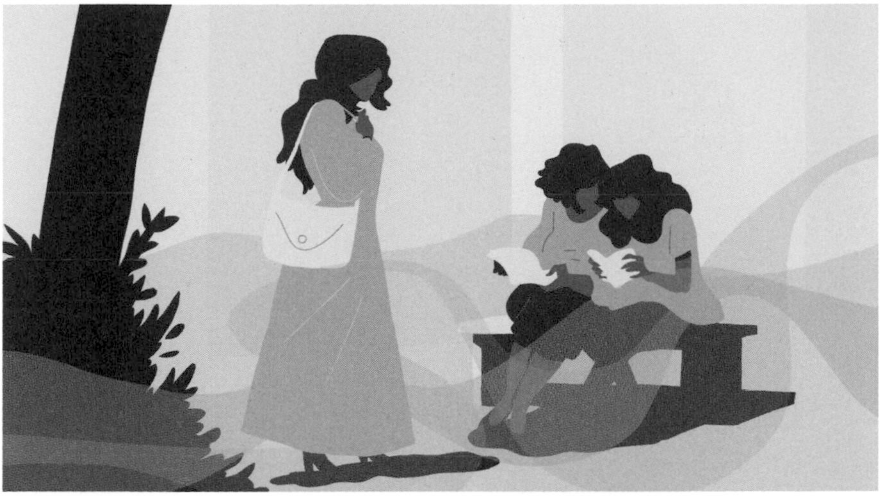

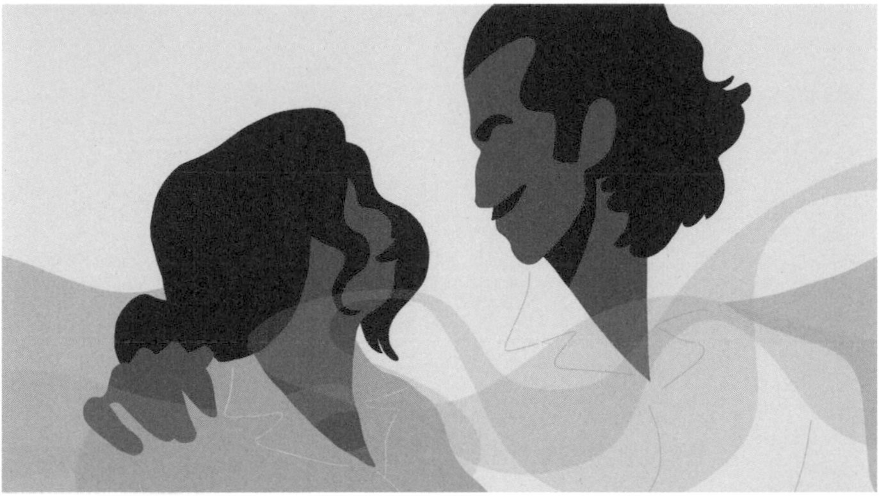

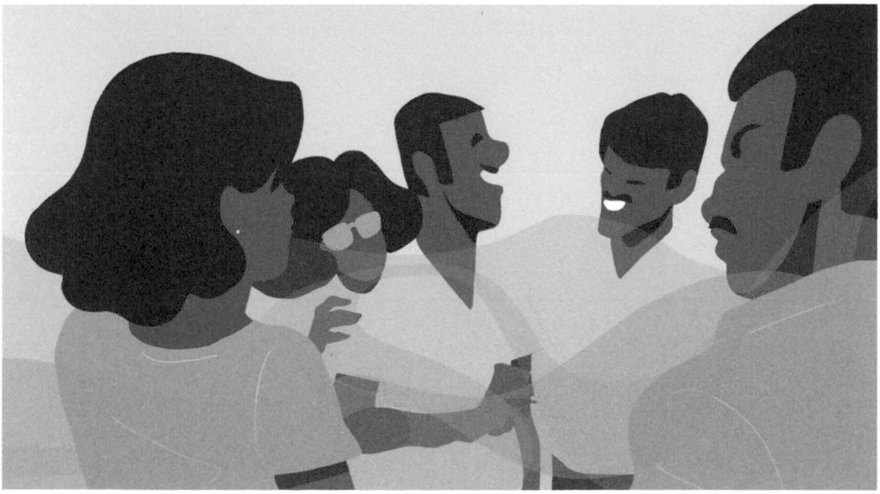

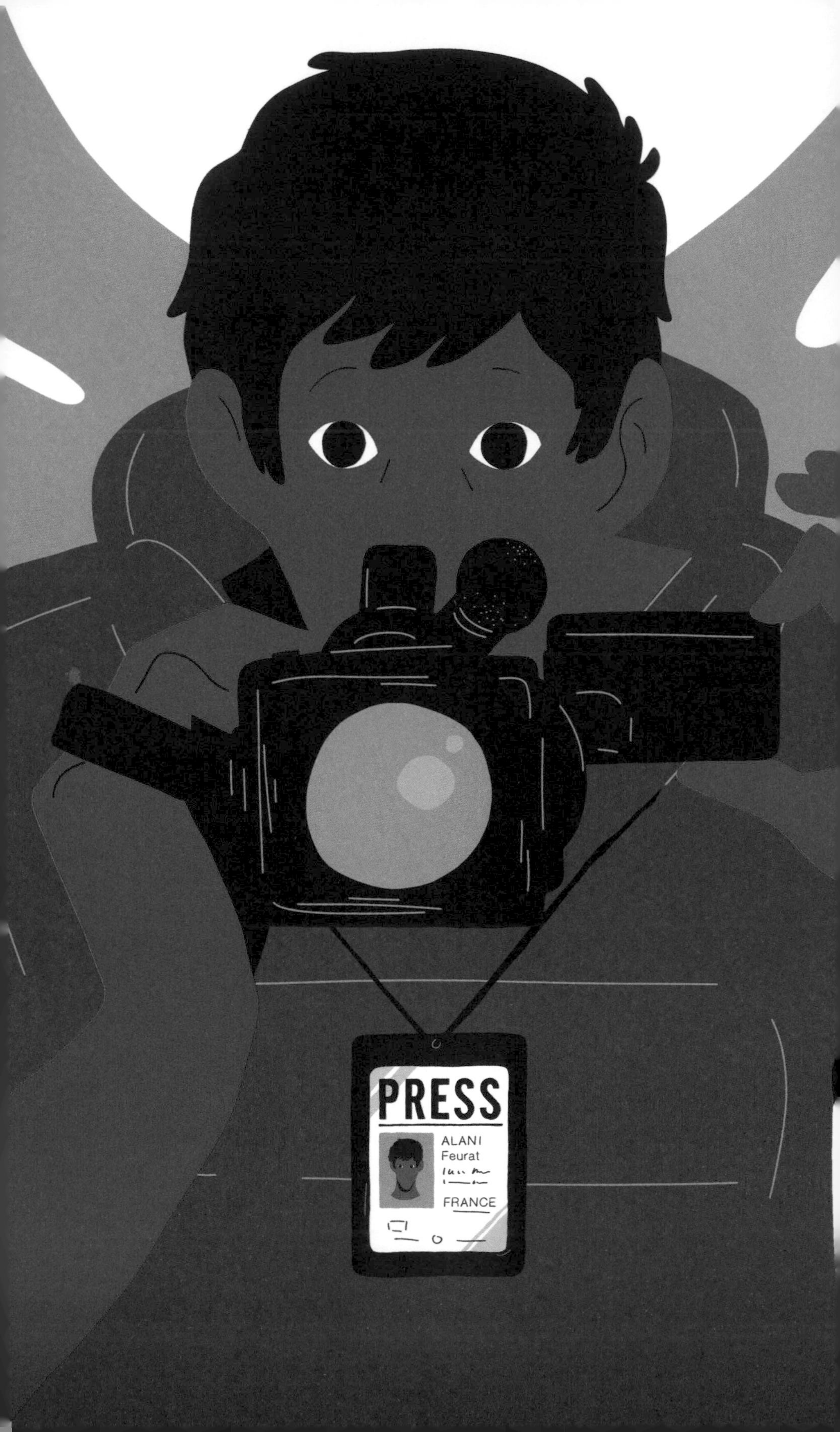
PRESS
ALANI
Feurat
FRANCE

2006–2007   **Syria, a country at peace. A stable country back then. A country where the media had no worries. A wonderful country.**

801   Amman is the Rome of the Middle East, built on seven hills. It's a second Iraq. 20% of its population comes from a country at war.

802   And this has caused inflation to soar in recent years. Iraqis came with a lot of cash and bought apartments.

803   Many lament the influx from neighboring states. Nonetheless, it's a country of refugees. 60% of the population is of Palestinian origin.

804   With the recent arrival of Syrians, the Jordanians are a minority. Strange situation. But it's a relatively stable country.

805   I'm there for several days, staying with one of my aunts. She fled Iraq, and, like the others, probably won't return. "Maybe never."

806   Amman gives me an opportunity to meet with tribal leaders and officials. Jordan is their sometimes forced weekend getaway. *Shaykh* Tarek is there.

807   He's a businessman originally from the village of Halabsa just ten kilometers from Fallujah. Fallujah is surrounded by the American army.

808   Now Fallujah residents are scanned by the American army. They even had categories for the badges. "A" meant harmless. "C" meant terrorist.

809   I'm there to tell the story of the tribal "awakening." Armed young men financed by the American administration in the fight against al-Qaeda.

810   *Shaykh* Tarek can help me because he is involved. My uncle Fawzi, who was the governor of Kout in the 1980s, is with me when I meet with him.

811   The meeting is scheduled at the headquarters of *Shaykh* Tarek, just north of the third roundabout. In Amman, locations are determined by district and the nearest roundabout.

812   We are greeted by a member of the Halbusi tribe. A young man in a suit with slicked-back hair and a very black mustache.

813   The *shaykh*, a tall guy, also wearing a suit, has a deep, soft voice. We sit down on the black leather sofa.

814   I brought along a camcorder I purchased with my meager earnings as a freelancer. A Sony PD170 with DV cassettes (now ancient technology).

815   I want to interview the *shaykh* but also talk to him about my work. Surely he can get me an in with his men in Fallujah.

816   We talk about al-Qaeda and about Sunni representation in Baghdad. In 2007, the political system there was already corrupt.

817   The conversation ends. My uncle, who is always in a rush, pays his respects to the *shaykh*. Now is my chance. I ask him for five minutes.

818   My uncle knows nothing about my plans. He's waiting outside. This is not customary, but I don't have a choice. The *shaykh* puffs his cigar.

Iraq's Tribal *Sahwa*
الصحوة
Arabic for "Awakening," the *Sahwa* was a mobilization of Arab tribes in cooperation with US forces in Iraq to drive al-Qaeda out of Iraq.

819   I get right to the point. "I want to go to Fallujah to film the tribal #*Sahwa*." He smiles and takes a puff while watching me. "OK."

820   "I have a car leaving in two days. There will be five of you. Rendezvous at 3 a.m." He knows I want discretion. My uncle is waiting. I take my leave.

821 Amman at 2:30 a.m. A moonless sky. Everyone is asleep at Aunt Khamael's. I'm sitting on the sofa. My suitcase is packed.

822 No one knows I'm going to Fallujah. Here's an ironic twist: to reassure my family, I tell them I'm going to Syria.

823 Syria, a country at peace. A stable country back then. A country where the media had no worries. A wonderful country. A sister country.

824 In short, I had to lie to my family so that I could go to Fallujah without any drama. Only Marc Berdugo at the CAPA press agency in Paris knows my plan.

825 I had been to see him with my Sony. "I'm leaving for Fallujah soon, any interest?" He looked at me for a bit and smiled at me. He said yes.

826 I liked Marc Berdugo right from the start. Saying yes to a twenty-seven-year-old kid with no television experience was brave (or crazy).

827 We shook hands and he wished me luck. And now I'm at my aunt Khamael's at three in the morning, my suitcase packed, excited but nervous.

828 Men I don't know are waiting for me in the Jebel district of Amman. I arrive on time, and three men stow their suitcases.

829 "Salam aleykom ya Fourat!" A warm greeting. One of the members of the Halbusi tribe looks exactly like the "Arab" in *Tintin*.

830 A red *keffieh*. A blue *dishdasha*. They get in the front. I'm in the back next to *shaykh* Salam. He has the charisma of an up-and-coming leader. "Bismillah!"

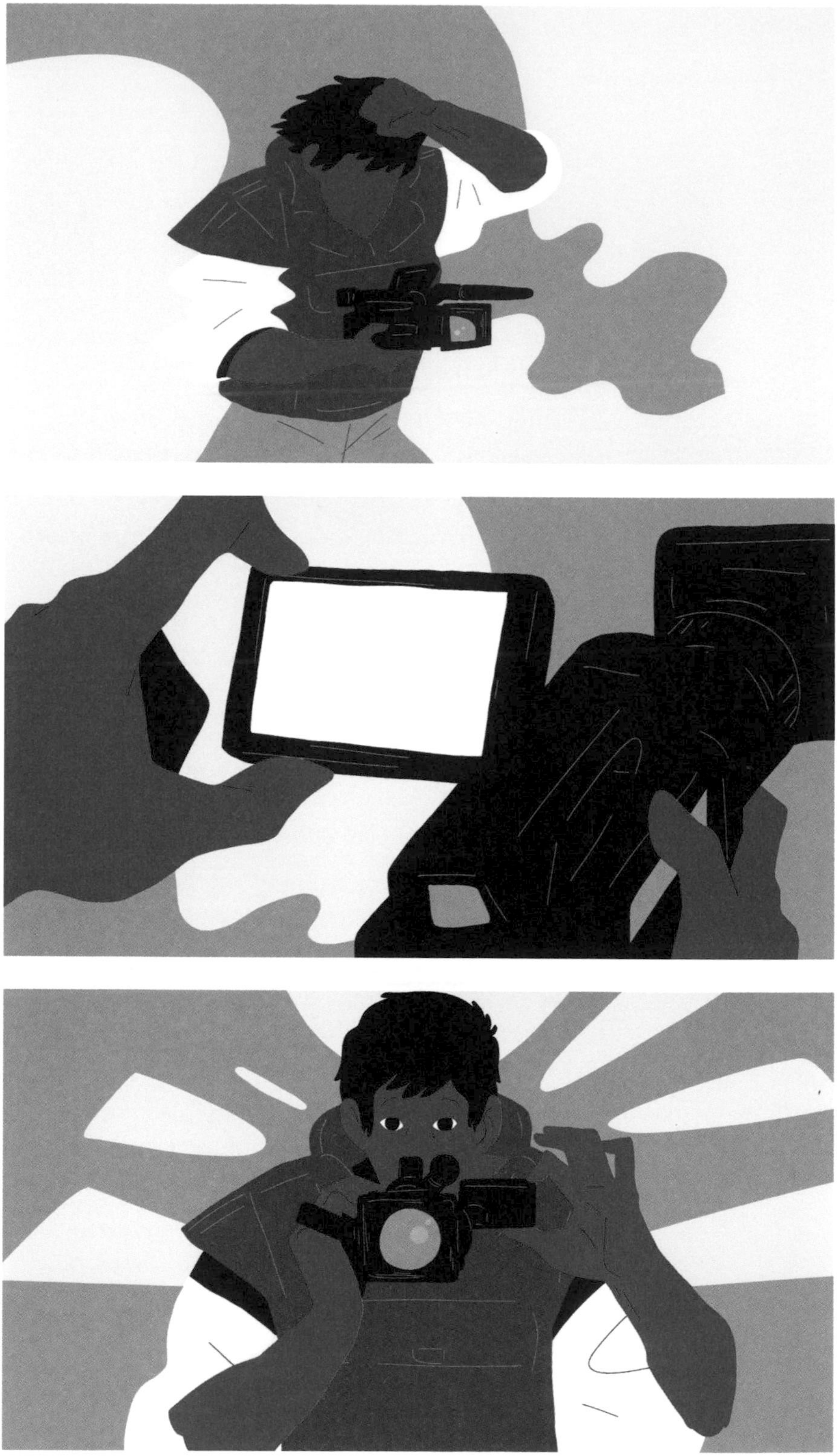

831 At the border, a member of the Halbusi tribe offered us tea and stamped our passports posthaste.

832 I press the on button and use manual focus. *Shaykh* Salam's face becomes sharp. It's 10 o'clock in the morning and we're driving on the Iraqi side.

833 *Shaykh* Salam's face is sharp against the desolate background of al-Anbar province. The road, too, is deserted.

834 *Shaykh* Salam is talking about the *Sahwa*—the awakening. It's as if the tribes were asleep and then shaken awake by a nightmare called al-Qaeda.

835 Obviously it's more complicated than that. Up front, the Arab from *Tintin* has taken out his 9 mm. It's a dangerous road, especially on the way to Rutba at the 160 mark.

836 War is raging between the *Sahwa* militias and al-Qaeda in Iraq. The tribes have the upper hand. al-Qaeda has lost control of the cities.

837 But murders on one side or the other happen daily. Suicide bombs, car bombs. "An eye for an eye, and a tooth for a tooth."

838 We pass through Ramadi. *Shaykh* Salam phones his colleagues. A police car will be able to get me in without a badge.

839 The police liaison is waiting for me at the Fallujah checkpoint. A guy with a mustache flips on the siren. We're ushered through American security.

840 In Fallujah, my Sony PD170, on its maiden voyage, is already recording. I film everything. It's the start of a very long adventure.

841   We stop at the home of Abu Younis, a member of the Albu Alwan tribe. He lives in the Mohandessin district, is the same age as me, and will be my guide.

842   Abu Younis is a former soccer player. A tall athletic guy with pale eyes, he joined the Awakening because "there's no other work."

843   He's surrounded by a cohort of youths. They all want to come with me. We head out in a three-car convoy toward downtown.

844   The market is teeming with people. The land-scape chaotic. There's not a single building that hasn't been shot up. Many are half standing or in a heap.

845   With Omar, one of the young men, we drive along the Euphrates to the right of the green bridge. Florists squat by their crates to water them.

846   Across the way, there's a bathhouse called "Fourat." The road along the river winds toward downtown, leading to a former synagogue.

847   The synagogue has been turned into a primary school. Along the road there are checkpoints for the police and the *Sahwa*—all very young men.

848   No one knows I'm here, but word travels fast. I'm filming and so I'm quite conspicuous. Abu Younis drives me to a friend's house.

849   He has a music store. Hundreds of records on the walls. He reopened after the *Sahwa* arrived. Al-Qaeda doesn't allow music.

850   His name is Mohamed and he is smiling but looks a little stressed. He plays an Iraqi music mix by the popular artist Hussam al-Rassam.

851 Fallujah is in a terrible state. It looks like it's been hit by an earthquake. Everything is gray. Covered in dust.

852 Even the face of this young man who just greeted me is dusty. His name is Qatada. His life revolves around doing business. A bundle of energy.

853 The incarnation of resourcefulness, he takes advantage of every opportunity that comes his way. He does odd jobs. He's a survivor.

854 Qatada takes me by the hand and leads me to a shop. He calls over the guy wielding a tray who serves the tea.

855 The teapot makes its rounds for tea service. My camcorder is rolling, teaspoons are stirring, the minutes are ticking by.

856 Now it's Abu Younis's turn to take me somewhere. Just next door to a photography studio. The al-Salam Studio, a small shop on the corner.

857 We go inside. Greetings are exchanged. A young man sitting in front of a computer looks up to say hello. "Are you the Frenchman?"

858 "Everyone is talking about the Frenchman in Fallujah with his camcorder." Mohamed saw me the day before filming at a stop light.

859 He looks more closely at me. Like he had just discovered electricity. "You know, I have an aunt who lives in France."

860 "Her name is Wafa al-Jumaili." I stand there, mouth agape. Then I respond: "That's my mother!" I just discovered a maternal cousin.

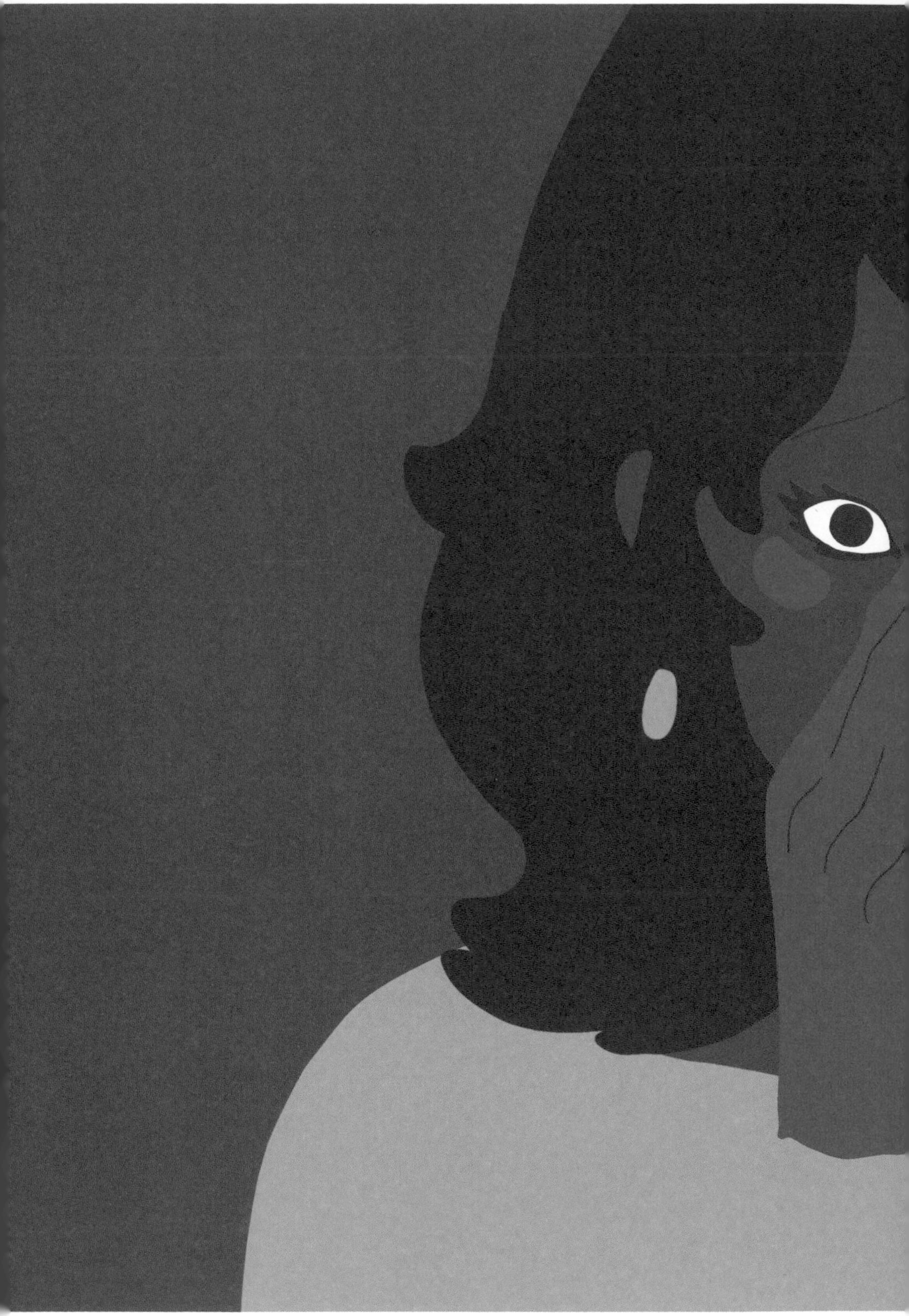

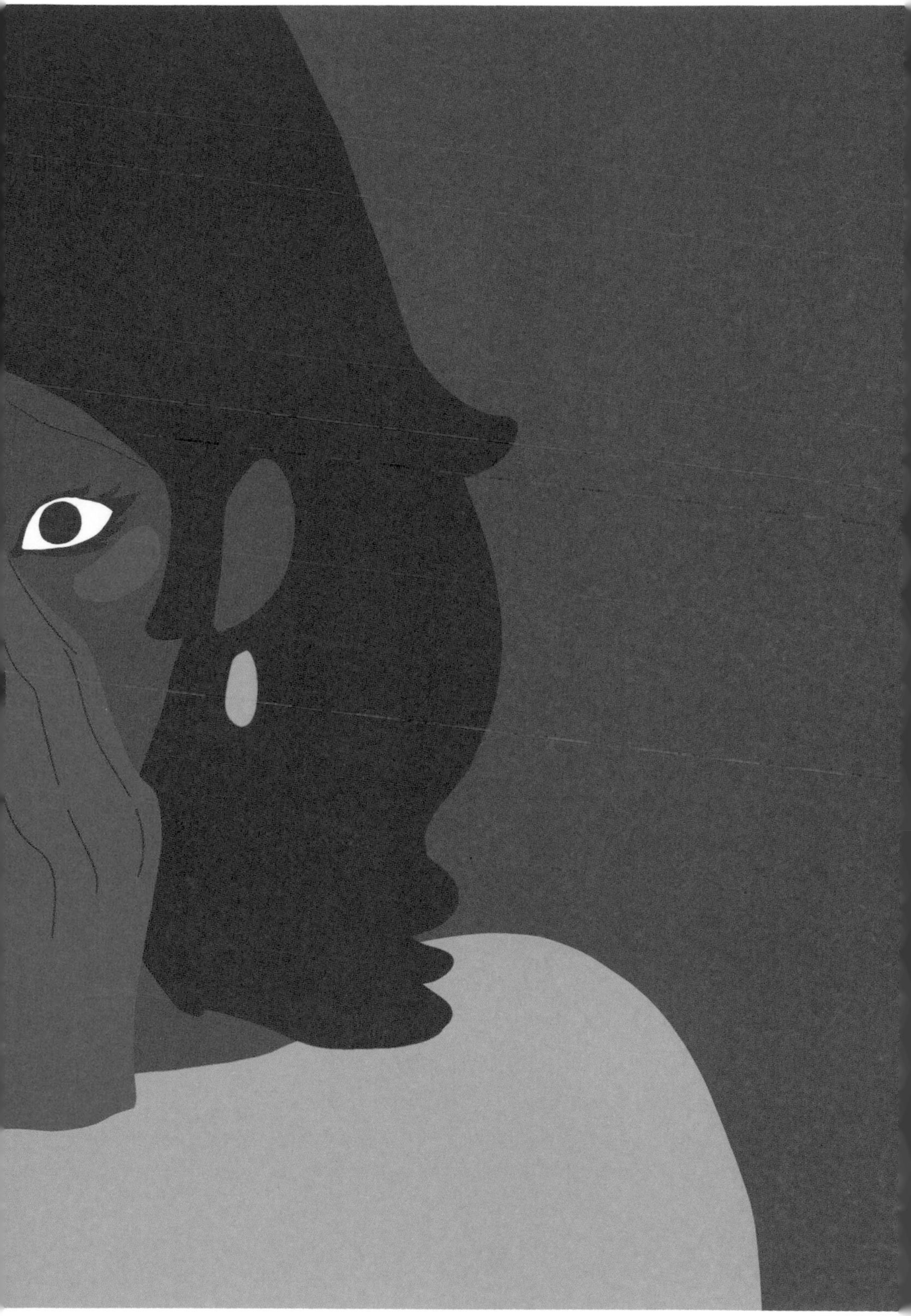

861 It's one of the most wonderful chance meetings. Mohamed calls his two brothers, Mahmud and Ahmed. They run into the studio. We hug.

862 Abu Younis is as surprised as I am. He thought he was introducing me to his friends, but this is my family at the al-Salam Studio.

863 My mother, the youngest of four sisters, has three half brothers. I had never met them, but I knew they existed.

864 I just met the children of my uncle Moayed. They invite me to their place that evening. Abu Younis, who instigated this happy coincidence, comes with me.

865 The Mohandessin district. An immense and magnificent house, with a living room as large as five Parisian studios. An uncle who is shorter than me.

866 He's standing there, with a pointy mustache reminiscent of earlier days, a cigar in his left hand and a smile in the right corner of his mouth. Uncle Moayed.

867 We embrace. "How is your mother?" Then: "What are you doing in Iraq?" Then: "What is your line of work?" Me: "Journalist." Him: "Why?"

868 He looks at me with sadness. "Why waste your time on that? The only thing that matters, nephew, is the dollar!" I don't know what to say.

869 My cousins told me about my uncle's depression. Ever since 2003 and the free fall of Iraq, he no longer goes out. He drinks. He cries.

870 He's no longer a man of his time. The world has passed him by, and he remains stuck in the golden age of Iraq, now long gone. An Iraq that is no more.

871 There are only men in this room. And weapons. Cigarettes. A deck of cards. We play a popular card game in Iraq: rummy.

872 Some want to hear the story of my chance meeting with my cousins in the photography studio. They're wide-eyed as they listen.

873 My cousins have two sisters. I won't see them until the guests leave. In Fallujah, women are neither seen nor mentioned.

874 Apparently Mohamed wants me to sleep here. Abu Younis tries to discourage that, but he gives up. "Family first" is the final argument.

875 Upstairs, my cousins surround me and pepper me with questions about France, about my life there. Their questions are endearing.

876 They talk about the photography studio. Mohamed is a real geek. He works on retouching photos: "Even the ugliest ones come out beautifully."

877 What works best? Romantic landscapes. A young married man with his wife. Mohamed superimposes floral embellishments.

878 It looks like the married couple has been on some grand voyage, even though they haven't left Fallujah. The photography studio is a fixture in the city. Business is good.

879 "Under al-Qaeda, it was different." Mohamed is not won over by the *Sahwa*, because they're an American solution to the problem.

880 Tomorrow I'll attend a *fasil*, a tribal council, a parallel system of justice where they settle disputes: money, murder, a goat that's been hit by a car.

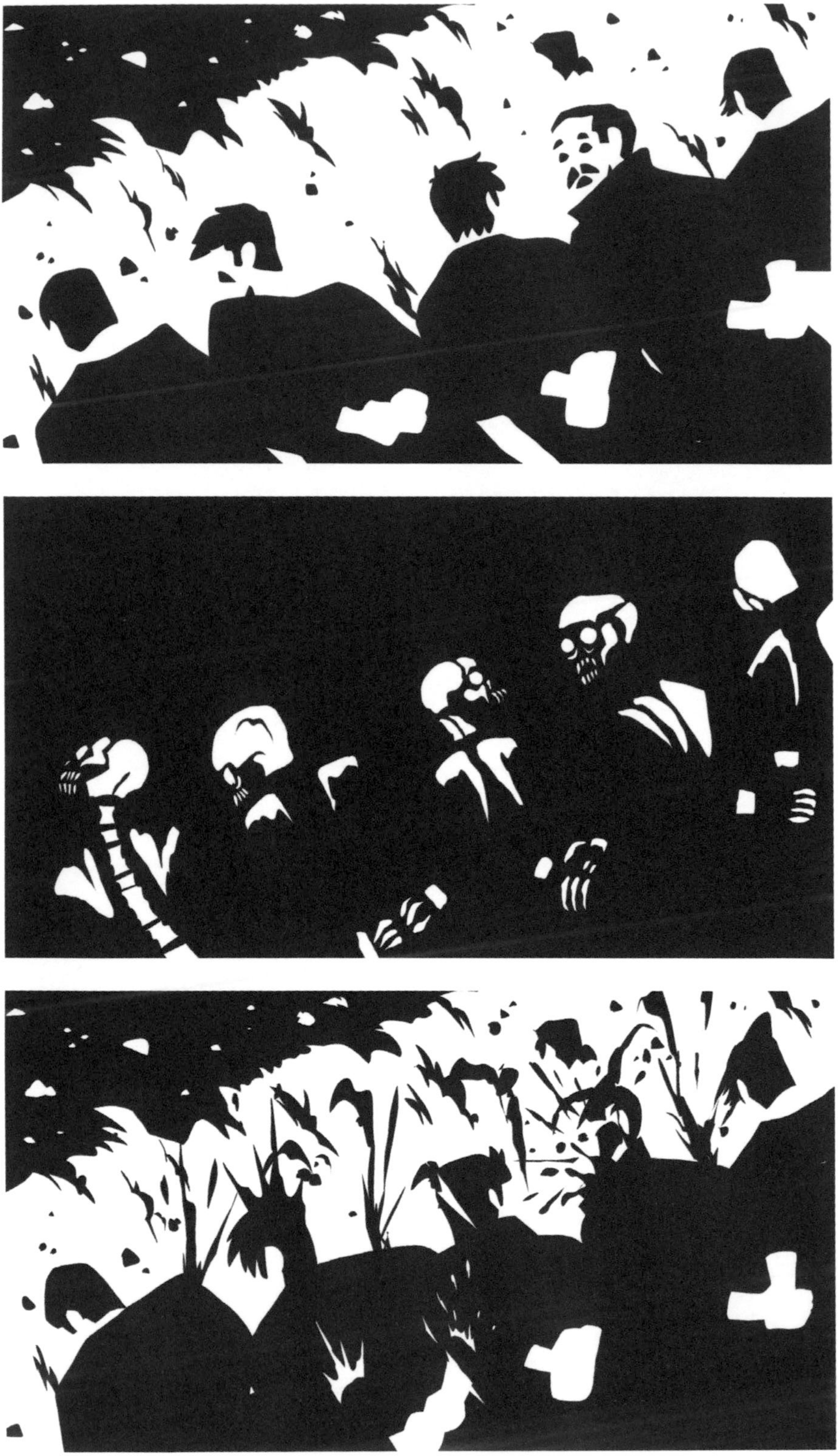

881　We're in Karma, the stronghold of the Jumaili tribe. About forty *shuyukh* (the plural of *shaykh*) are waiting patiently.

882　Cups of coffee are passed around. My camcorder is rolling. I don't want to miss the entrance of the defendant. This is a courtroom.

883　A tribal tribunal. *Fasil.* When the state no longer exists, the tribe is there. Today is an important meeting. Tensions are high.

884　A man enters the room, head down. He is handcuffed and surrounded by two members of his own tribe. They introduce him.

885　"You asked us to bring Brahim to you. Here is Brahim." It's judgment time for the people. The men look at him, drinking their coffee.

886　They have Brahim sit on the floor. A *fasil* brings together two tribes—that of the victim and that of the accused. A *shaykh* of a third tribe passes judgment.

887　Brahim is accused of having shot a member of the other tribe. He is strongly suspected of being a member of al-Qaeda in Iraq.

888　The *shaykh* of the third tribe launches into a fierce monologue: "We're going to do to Brahim what he did to Q.: we're going to shoot him three times."

889　Then follows a discussion between the two tribes. They offer some context. Then they ask: "How many missions have you carried out?" "Only one!"

890　Brahim: "I swear that was the only mission. I've never killed anyone, whether Sunni or Shiite."

891 Brahim: "It's the *shaykh* who gives the orders. He tells us what to do, who to shoot. We don't know why."

892 The *shaykh* intervenes: "Who is this *shaykh*?" Brahim: "They call him "the shaykh." We don't know who he is. He gives us orders, and that's it."

893 Voices rise in the room. The debate becomes heated. Argument is met with argument. He didn't kill him, but the victim is seriously injured.

894 "Qisas!" some cry. *Qisas* means "vengeance" or "an eye for an eye." I can't believe what I'm filming here.

895 The tribes reach a proposed settlement. Brahim's tribe will buy back his freedom for 10,000 dollars. This sum will cover the costs of the victim's surgery.

896 To reach this special deal, Brahim was questioned by the third tribe. He gave up valuable information on al-Qaeda. It has been recorded.

897 Sitting there blindfolded, on his knees, Brahim was interrogated for hours. This is my first encounter with a member of al-Qaeda.

898 We get up to leave, Abu Younis and I. It's a routine turn of events for him. But I'm still taken aback by what I just witnessed.

899 This is an example of what renowned sociologist Ibn Khaldun called *asabiyya*. Social cohesion. An absent state.

900 Civilization is built on the competition between tribe and state. *Fasil* is one example of this. We return to Fallujah.

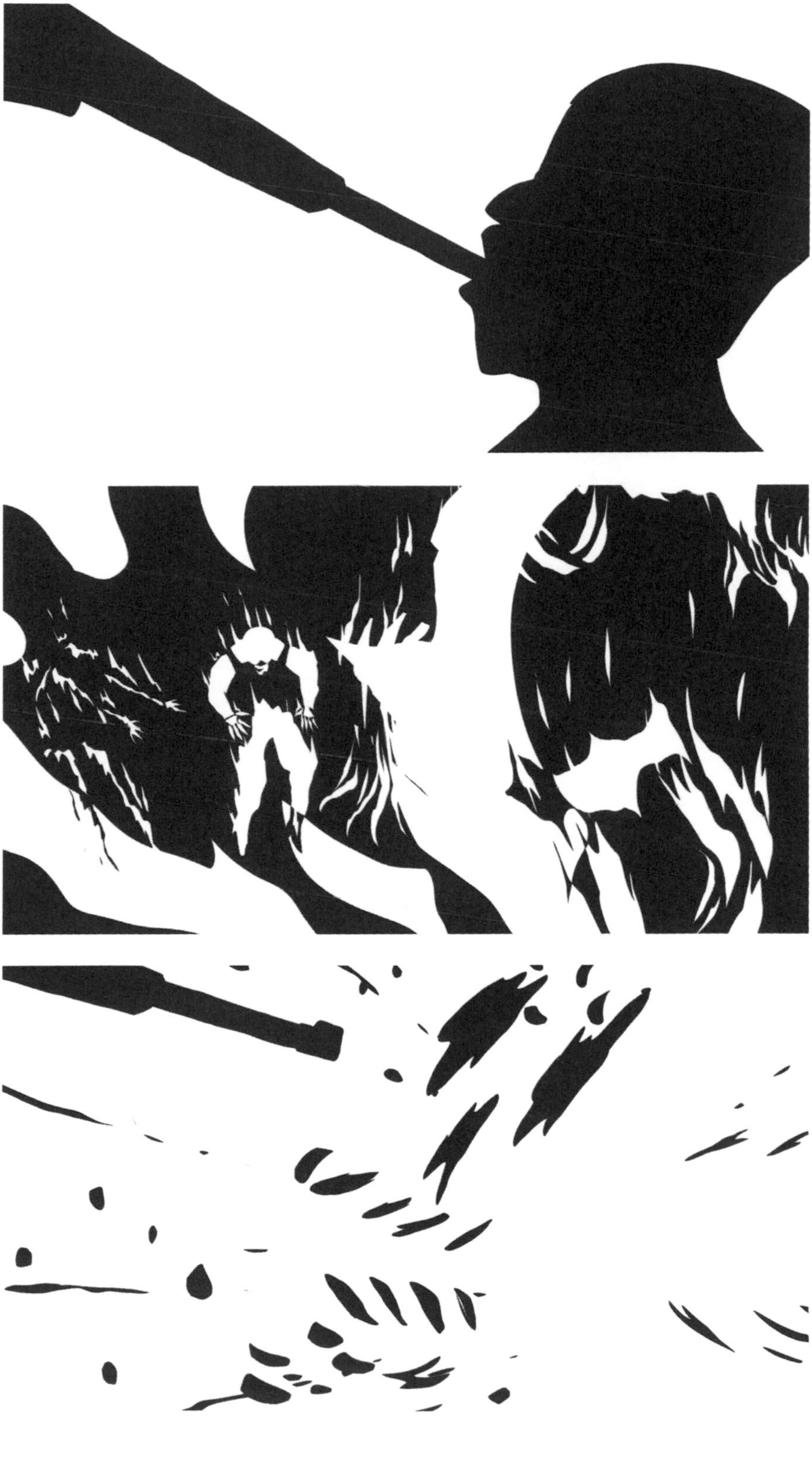

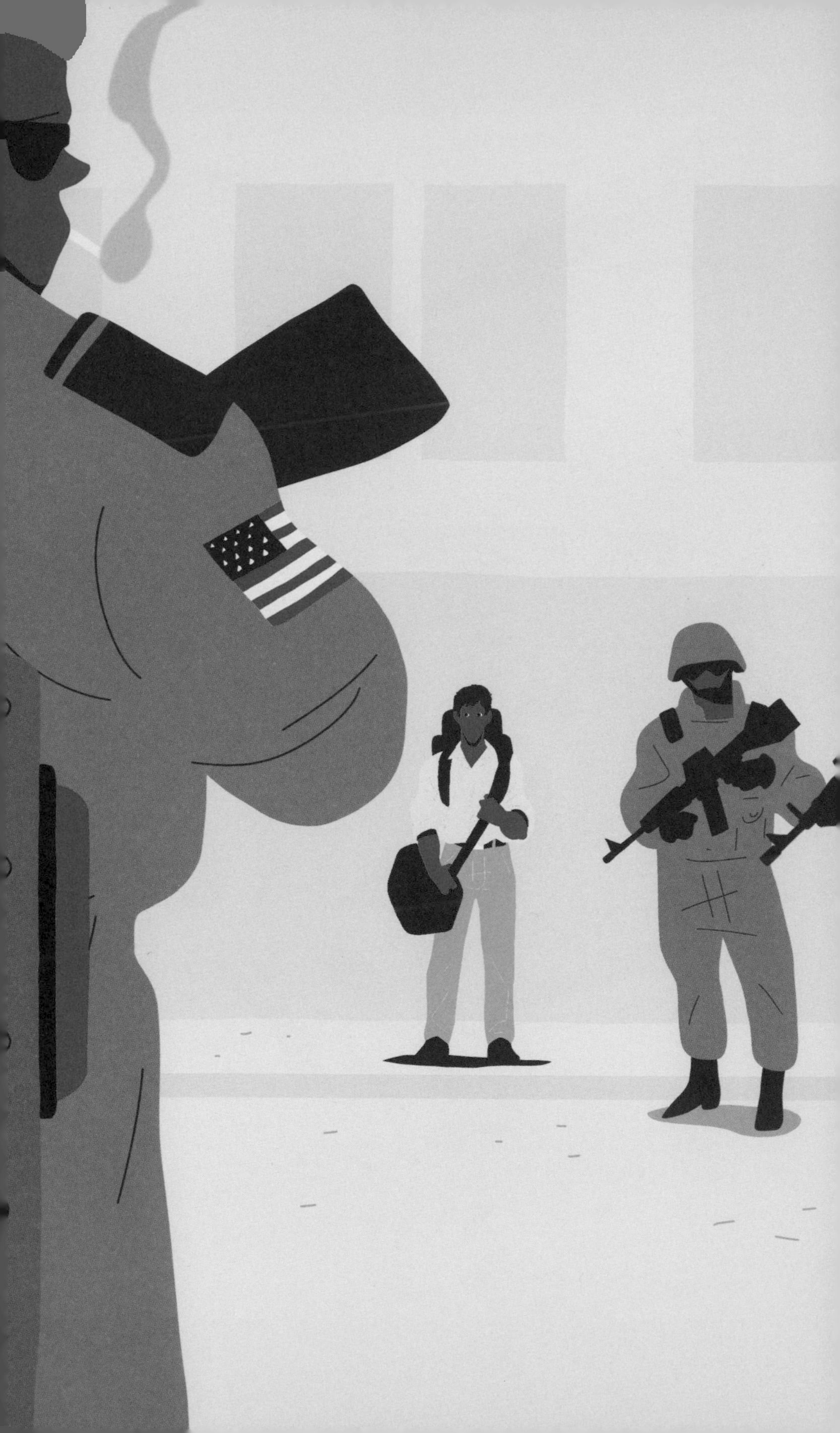

One evening, I summon the courage to tell them: "I'm an Iraqi." They're curious and flood me with questions.

901 The next day, Abu Younis takes me to the north Fallujah police station. It's controlled by a Jumaili, from my maternal tribe.

902 There's an American tank at the entrance. The precinct is co-managed with the Americans. Looks like I'm going to cross paths with them . . . and I'm not here legally.

903 We take the long, barbed-wire corridor. Here's a checkpoint. There are two young Fallujis with cigarettes dangling from their lips. I film them. They pose proudly.

904 We get to the door of the precinct. American soldiers are milling about. In response to each "Hey, journo, wut up?" I shoot back "Hey, man. . . ."

905 They're all the same age as me. Inside, I come across one guy sitting on a desk. I want to ask him some questions. It's okay, because he's "fucking bored."

906 I ask him if it frightens him being posted in such a dangerous city. He responds: "Hey man, Fallujah is now safer than Philadelphia now."

907 I don't get much from him. He says only that he's bored and that, thanks to the Jumaili police chief, things are going better in Fallujah.

908 As it happens, the chief is sitting in the office next door. Trimmed mustache, a bit of a paunch, dark-skinned. He sits up straight. Proud.

909 He says that all of the al-Qaeda members in the area are known to them. And that if they killed just one Iraqi, that situation would change.

910 "We flushed them all out one by one. The rest fled to neighboring towns. Only a couple dozen remain, mostly in Jolan."

911 Jolan is the largest district in Fallujah. Also the most popular. Two of my paternal uncles live there. I make an impromptu visit.

912 Everyone here knows one another. So I ask for directions to Hadji Ayad's house. "It's the house over there, on the left." I see it. Abu Younis follows me.

913 On the way, I come across a teenager. Tall and thin. I ask if this is Hadji Ayad's house. "Yes, he's my father." Smile.

914 I ask him if he knows who I am. Smiling, he blurts out "Feurat?" I respond "Ahmed?" Now Abu Younis is smiling.

915 That small, smooth step in front of the house is still there. Inside, the chicken coup is still there. My uncle Ayad is there, he stands up.

916 Greetings. Abu Younis follows me into the living room. My uncle hasn't really changed a bit, except for the glasses on his nose. "Allah aboulkheyr!"

917 I tell him why I've come. He nods his head. The presence of the young members of the *Sahwa* seems to make him uncomfortable. I realize my mistake.

918 My uncle is a veteran. He'll never collaborate with the Americans. He remains polite but is a bit terse with Abu Younis.

919 Abu Younis places his revolver on the table in the living room. My uncle, a ranking officer in the army, doesn't appreciate that.

920 There are three kinds of clashes here. Generational. Political. Social. The old vs. the young. City residents vs. villagers. *Mujahidin* vs. *Sahwa*.

921 I decide to stay the night in Jolan with Uncle Ayad. Abu Younis and the others return home with the plan of picking me up in the morning.

922 My uncle Ayad is smiling again. My other uncles have come to see me. Uncle Emad, the poet, is there with a letter for my father.

923 It's a poem he wrote glorifying the Iraqi resistance in Fallujah. I put the letter in my backpack. I'll read it later.

924 The conversation centers on the current situation. For my uncles, the *Sahwa* is just a tool the Americans are using to crush the resistance.

925 Upon hearing this, Uncle Ayad's expression changes. I realize that veterans like him have been ostracized.

926 But what's most difficult is being under the command of the Americans. I notice that the curtains are closed on all the living room windows.

927 Each time an American convoy goes by, Uncle Ayad twists in pain, as if the anger is breaking his bones. He's sick at heart.

928 In 2004, he was one of the neighborhood leaders, known for his military acumen and his armed fight against the American occupiers.

929 He was still fighting them just a couple months ago. Three years of combat. Today, he is reduced to silence. I am his confidant.

930 He described two significant incidents he was involved in: a Hollywood face-off with the Americans and a large-scale operation.

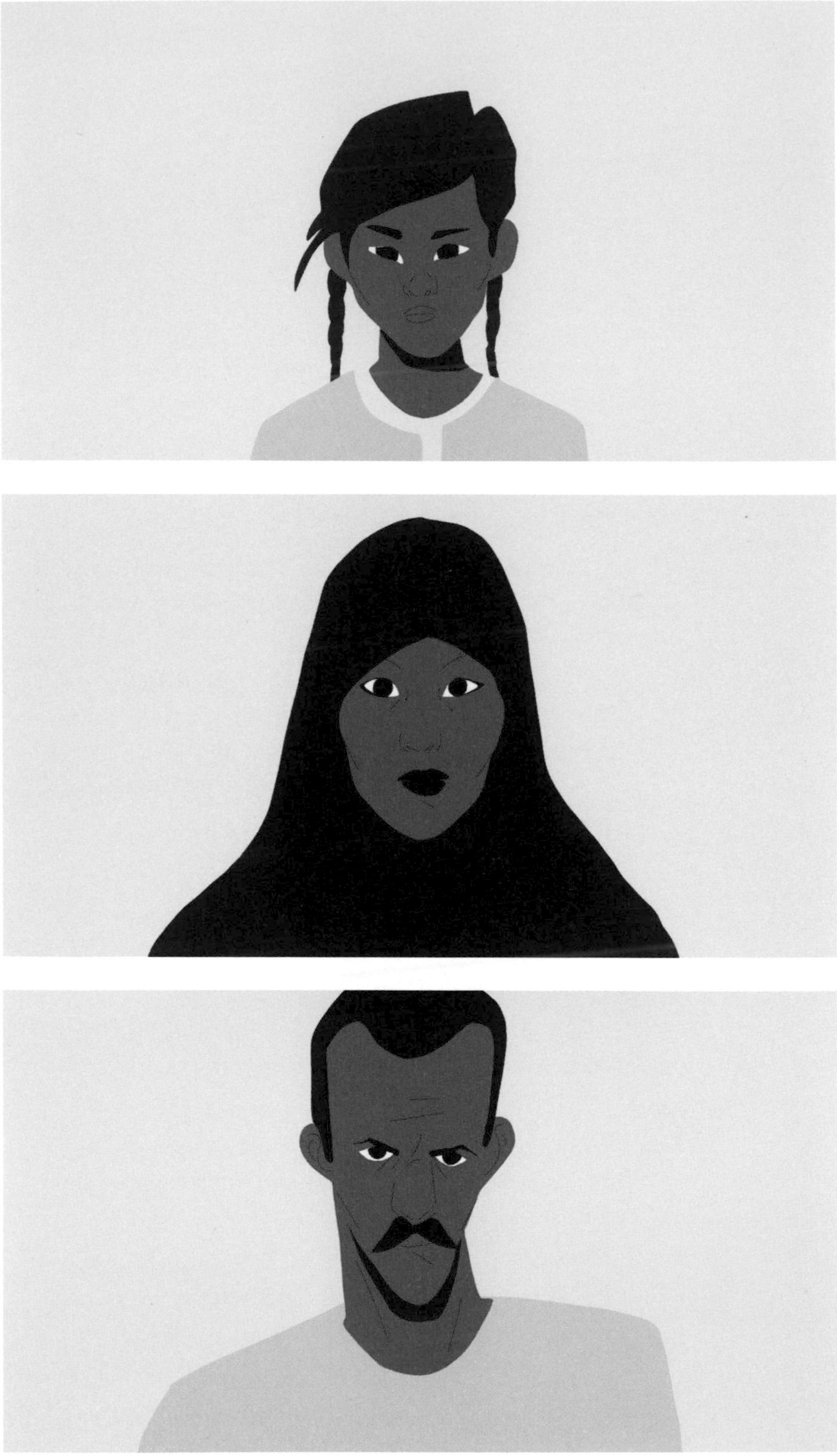

931   Uncle Ayad was the leader of a neighborhood group in Jolan. About ten men. Most of them shopkeepers during the day and masked fighters at night.

932   Among them was a Kurd from Fallujah. Before the war, thousands of Kurds lived here, generation after generation. Real Fallujis.

933   Uncle Ayad takes me to visit the Kurd. He's wearing eyeglasses and evidently lost a leg in combat. His home is very modest.

934   With shining eyes, he talks about my uncle. "We told him to run when they started shooting, but he just slowly walked through the gunfire."

935   One day, he, my uncle, and a third man came face-to-face with an American patrol. Heavy suspense, like in a war film.

936   Simultaneously comic and tragic: The Kurd drops his Kalashnikov. The American soldiers start shooting, striking my uncle twice.

937   The third man fires a dushka from the back of the pickup truck. They take off in a squeal of tires. The Americans quickly scatter.

938   My uncle shows me the bullet scars. One on his left hand and the other on his lower back. He has a slight limp.

939   I wonder if my uncle killed any American soldiers. I don't dare ask him directly. He understands and answers "Allah yaalem,"—"God knows."

Hadji
الحجّي
A person who has made the pilgrimage to Mecca.

940   He is well respected in the neighborhood. When people greet him, they call him *Hadji*. He made the pilgrimage to Mecca in 2007.

941   The second story is the one about a large-scale operation.My uncle Ayad described exactly what happened.

942   It had to do with a planned ambush of the man in charge of the war in Iraq in 2004: the American four-star general John Abizaid.

943   According to my uncle, different armed groups would collaborate in 2004 on special operations of high importance.

944   At the time, members of the al-Qaeda military could include Iraqi ex-officers like my uncle, for instance.

945   The case my uncle Ayad was involved in was a large-scale operation targeting an elite American convoy that was carrying Abizaid.

946   This was February 2004. Dozens of groups had prepared for this ambush. From al-Qaeda to national-ists, including my uncle.

947   Uncle Ayad was at the forefront. He describes the violence of the surprise attack on a convoy of dozens of American and Iraqi armored vehicles.

948   His eyes are shining when he tells the story. He recounts the obvious panic of the soldiers and Abi-zaid being escorted away.

949   "The general fell on his backside. He was picked up by soldiers and thrown into a Humvee before racing off. A close call."

950   My uncle and the others knew that Abizaid was there. How did they obtain this information if not from the Iraqi police? I never got an answer.

951 Abu Younis picks me up the next day. He wants to show me something. They're photos he got from some neighbors.

952 With a solemn expression, he tells me there's a real problem in Fallujah ever since the battle in 2004. Babies are being born completely deformed.

953 The photos are horrible. There are babies with twisted legs. Others without arms. Some without eyes. I had never seen anything like it.

954 Doctors at the Fallujah hospital don't know what to do. They are overwhelmed, don't have the means, are completely ignored.

955 I find it hard to believe that three years after the Battle of Fallujah no one is investigating these kinds of congenital anomalies.

956 I put all the photos in my bag and get as many details as possible. Abu Younis is counting on me to get the word out. The hospital, too.

957 "You're from here, families will trust you, they will speak to you," says Abu Younis. It's a delicate subject. Taboo.

958 Families are ashamed to speak of their children born with physical disabilities. Most don't survive, but some are still alive. They grow up in the shadows.

959 Given the chaotic situation, the sectarian war, and the occupation, the health of Falluji children is not a priority in Baghdad.

960 I made a promise to myself that day to conduct a full investigation on the subject. It will take time, but I'll get an answer. *Inch'Allah*.

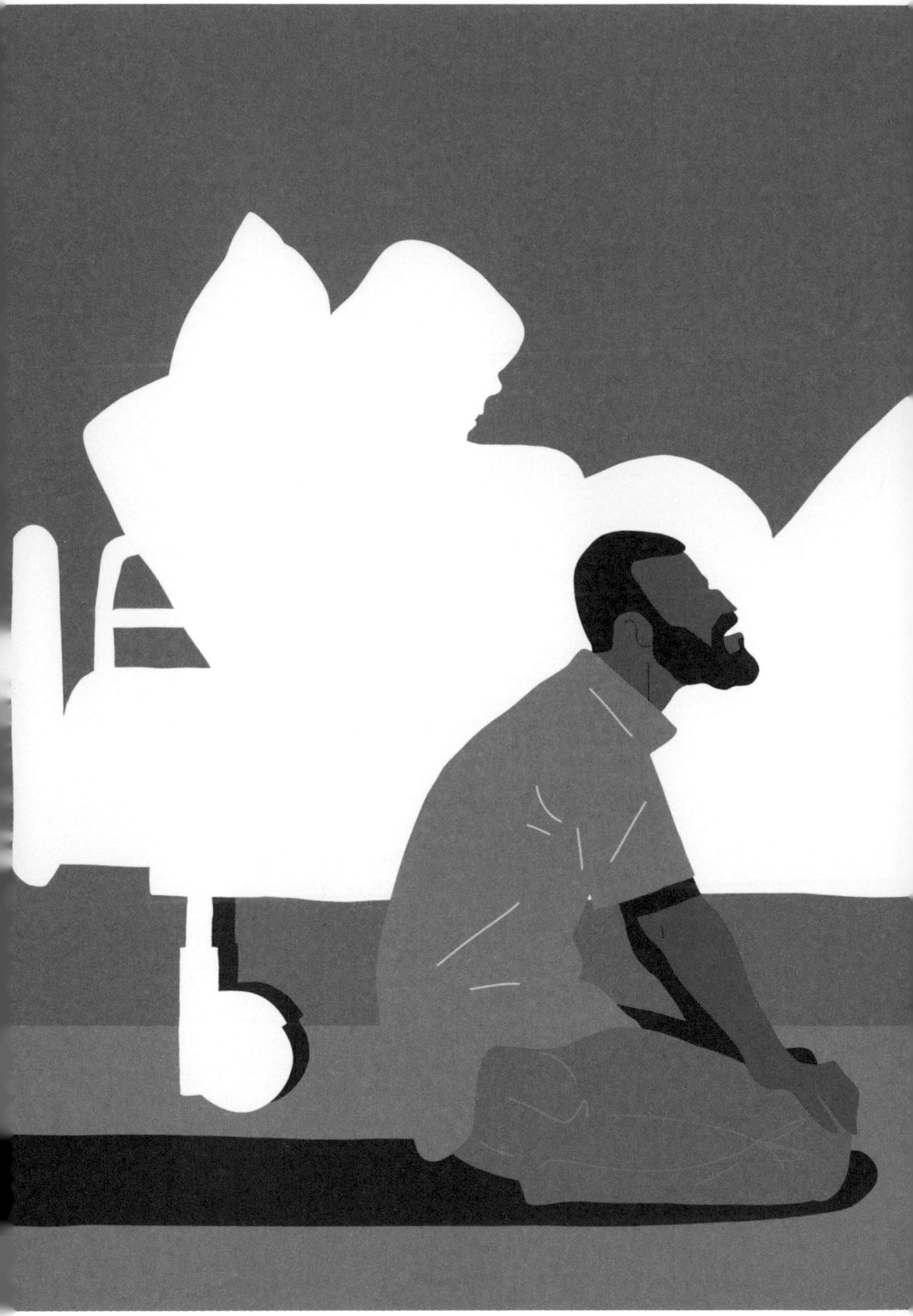

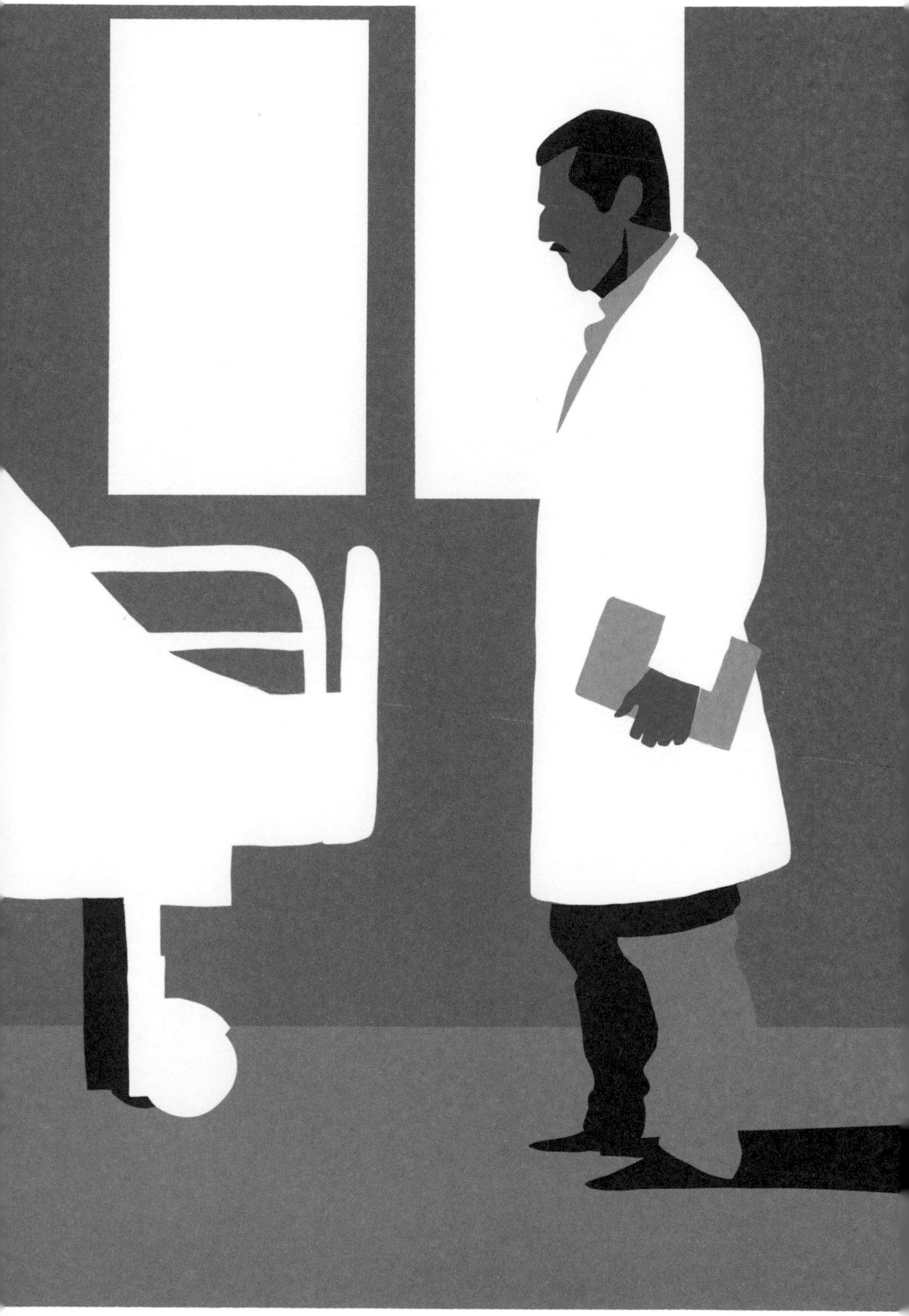

961 I see my uncle Ayad again a couple days before leaving Fallujah. There are two city bikes in the garden. One for him and one for me.

962 We ride around town on these bicycles. It's my uncle's preferred means of transport. He knows every street in every district.

963 When he's on a bike, he can avoid all the new checkpoints set up by the Iraqi police, the *Sahwa*, and the Americans.

964 After shopping at the market on 40th Street, we head back to Jolan. We stop near an elementary school.

965 This is where the Americans took up residence to surveil the roofs of houses.

966 Where the first peaceful protesters were taken out by American bullets. Where 19 people were killed because they were protesting.

967 Uncle Ayad shows me where this insurrection, began. Where a series of cultural misunderstandings came to a head and ended in division.

968 Uncle Ayad no longer fights. They try to recruit him, but he continues his peaceful way of life in Fallujah. He has changed. He is hard. Very hard.

969 We say goodbye without knowing whether we'll ever see each other again. A car hired by Abu Younis will take me to Amman and the land of #KingAbdullah.

970 With Abu Younis and the other young men, we strike a pose in the garden. One last photo. Everyone is armed. And smiling. Except me.

971 On the road to Jordan, in a taxi with two members of the Halabsa tribe, it's raining. The sky is gloomy, like Fallujah.

972 My camcorder and 23 cassettes are packed in my luggage. I have everything I need for my first television piece for broadcast on Canal+.

973 More importantly, I have a lot of messages to pass along to my father. And an important investigation to do on babies with congenital disabilities in Falllujah.

974 I feel remorse for leaving my family, once again. For leaving Abu Younis, with whom I have a close tribal friendship. I'll see you soon!

975 The desert is gray in the rain. The cold, like the smell of wet sand, is relentless. We cross the Iraqi border without any problems.

976 On the Jordanian side, it's more complicated. I'm stopped at the first checkpoint. A young French-Iraqi man traveling alone: it's suspect.

977 A young guard rifled through my suitcase, my wallet, my coat. He sees my twenty-three cassettes, the camcorder. His eyes widen.

978 I have the pleasure of being interviewed by the border officer in charge. He plays the nice guy. He found Uncle Emad's letter.

979 The letter mentions the "heros" of the Iraqi resistance. Then he finds the photo of me with my armed friends. Will this be the end of me?

980 The chief wants to see my cassettes. He chooses one at random. I hit play. A soccer match in Fallujah. The chief smiles. I can leave.

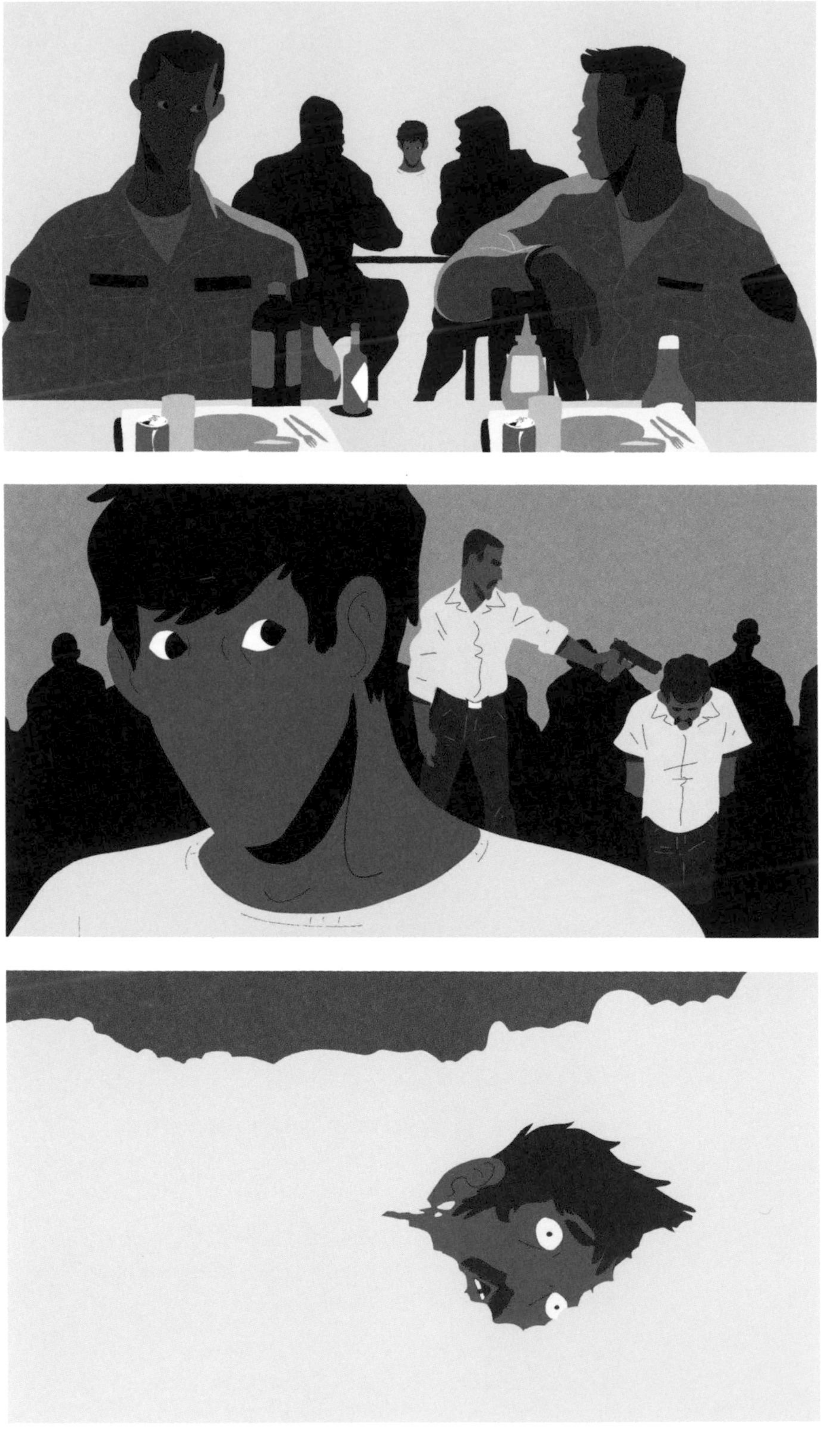

981 The next years pass in what feels like minutes. In 2008 American soldiers no longer walk in the streets. The convoys go by, and the Iraqis spit on them.

982 There is still the noise of Baghdad. Helicopters pass overhead in pairs. Gunshots wake us up and rock us to sleep.

983 There is still government corruption. Deals are made for the construction of walls and the purchase of unnecessary equipment.

984 There is still the question of oil. Iraqis don't see much of it. The state coffers grow. Hope dies.

985 As for me, I'm still there, too. Alone. My entire family on my mother's side has left Iraq. I move from house to house.

986 In 2009, the country is tinged black with oil and red with blood. For too long now, Iraq has sweated out a mixture of sulfur and hemoglobin.

987 Blood for oil. If Iraqis had had the choice, they would have given up oil for peace. What good is it to die on top of a gold mine?

988 What will be left of a nation without a state, a few months after the Americans pull out? Parcels of land around pipelines?

989 The Americans want to leave Iraq but only when the house is in order. The keys will be handed over to the oil companies.

990 Chinese, Turks, French, Italians, Russians will divvy up the oil fields that still function but are in very poor condition. Iraq is for sale.

991 In 2010, Iraq is following its descent into the maelstrom. "Yabooooooo!" At dawn I hear the cries of women, a common occurence in the neighborhood. A young man has died.

992 They're called "the weeping women." Women not necessarily from the family of the one who has died, who come to cry over the loss of a soul. To mourn.

993 A way to ward off evil, for sure. To pay homage to sorrow, to the loss of a life. To injustice that is now the law of the land.

994 Some, more reserved, choose to pay homage silently. Others feel the need to let their misfortune be heard. To cry out.

995 On this particular morning, their cries gave me goose bumps. The sight of these women dressed in black, of the casket on the ground, of the tears.

996 In 2011, just before the Americans pull out, I'm granted permission to film them one last time. A week in the Green Zone.

997 I have time to commiserate with them. Most of them are younger than me. At the beginning of the war, they would wander the streets of Baghdad. They would talk with the Iraqis.

998 After 5,000 deaths in their ranks, the soldiers no longer have contact with the people they're occupying. They leave the Green Zone only by helicopter or in armored vehicles.

999 During a conversation one evening, I summon the courage to tell them: "I'm an Iraqi." I was afraid I'd shut them down, but they are curious. Questions abound.

1000 "What's life like in Baghdad? What's the difference between Sunnis and Shiites? Between Arabs and Kurds?" Eight years after their arrival, they still don't know a thing. . . .

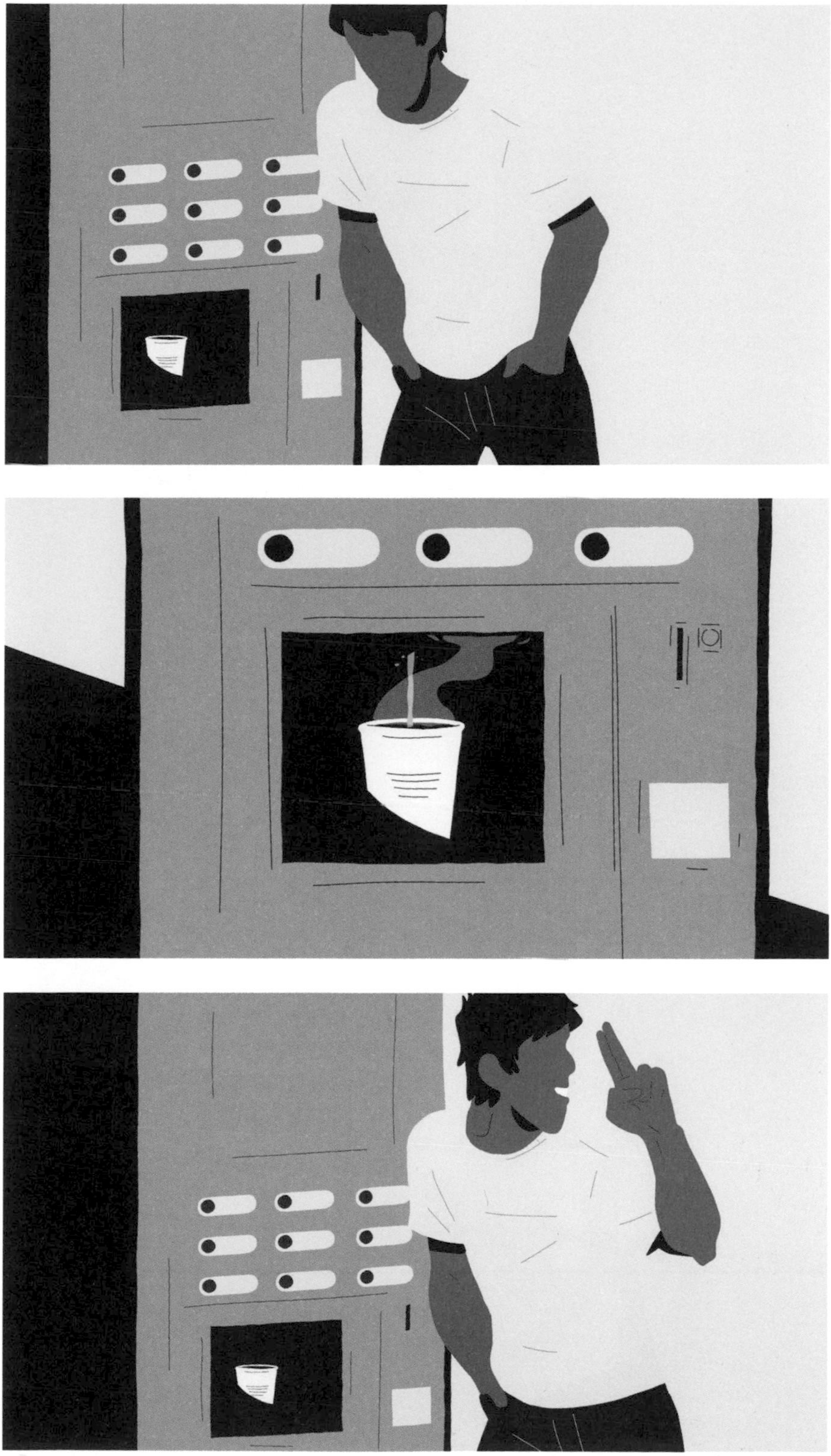

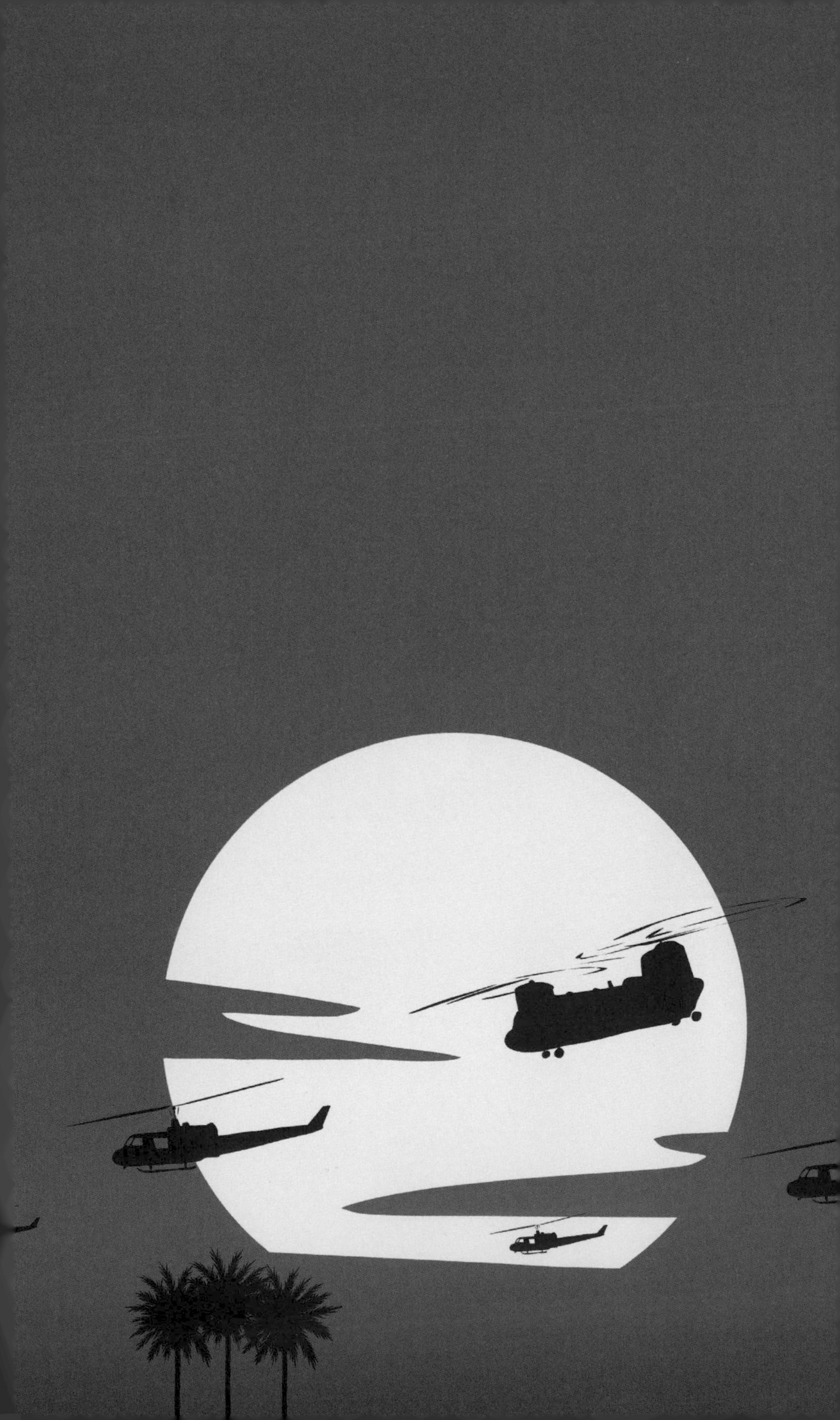

2011 Goodbye America!

Today, the country is in pieces. Divided. A war zone for armed factions backed by foreign powers.

This evening, I have an opportunity to look them in the eye and tell them exactly what I think. I tell them that freedom can't be forced. That in trying to kill one dictator, they have unleashed one thousand. That they have destroyed a country on account of a lie. That they have created this battlefield for armed factions backed by foreign countries that aren't really their allies. That they have done more harm than good. And that they actually had no business being here. That the Iraq I dreamed about as a child, the Iraq my father cherished, the Iraq traversed by the Euphrates River from which I get my name, is now lost to me forever.

This Iraq no longer exists.